P Goyen

Principles of English Composition through Analysis and Synthesis

A Text-Book for the Senior Classes of Elementary Schools...

P Goyen

Principles of English Composition through Analysis and Synthesis
A Text-Book for the Senior Classes of Elementary Schools...

ISBN/EAN: 9783744746649

Printed in Europe, USA, Canada, Australia, Japan

Cover: Foto ©Paul-Georg Meister /pixelio.de

More available books at **www.hansebooks.com**

PRINCIPLES

OF

ENGLISH COMPOSITION

THROUGH

ANALYSIS AND SYNTHESIS

A TEXT-BOOK FOR
THE SENIOR CLASSES OF ELEMENTARY SCHOOLS
AND FOR PUPIL-TEACHERS

BY

P. GOYEN

INSPECTOR OF SCHOOLS

London

MACMILLAN AND CO.

AND NEW YORK

1894

All rights reserved

PREFACE

As a means of teaching composition and the principles that govern sentence structure, analysis of sentences has completely broken down and become, outside the teaching profession, entirely discredited. Pupils parse and parse, analyse and analyse, for years of their school life, and in the end are ignorant of what constitutes a good sentence and wholly without ability to write one. The cause of this unsatisfactory result is not, I think, difficult to discover.

The parsing of single words, however well done, can be made to bear only on the syntax of single words—quite a trifle in sentence structure. Analysis, however, includes single words, phrases, and clauses—the whole mechanism of the sentence however complex, and, of course, ought to bear on the syntax of the whole mechanism; but unfortunately it has been made by the books to concern itself only with breaking down and classifying. Its sole aim has been to dismember the sentence and to place the *disjecta membra* under their appropriate headings. This is all very well from the point of view that decomposition and classification are the sole end of grammar; but ought they to be so regarded? Is not synthesis as important as analysis? Is it not necessary that the young student should be trained not only to decompose and classify, but also to *compose*, that is, to arrange words, phrases, and clauses in their most effective setting? Analysis is purely destructive; it destroys beauty of thought and beauty of form; synthesis restores both; it is the complement of analysis. This fact has been ignored by the text-books, and therefore analysis has become discredited. Analysis is useful chiefly for purposes of synthesis. From analysis the student learns to discern the parts and the function of the parts of the sentence; from synthesis and the rules of placement he learns to build up the sentence by placing the parts in their most effective setting.

In this little book analysis is treated only as a means to an end—the synthesis of sentences and the principles of sentence structure. No distinction is made between 'indirect object' and 'extension'; for whatever helps the predicate to express its meaning is an adjunct to the predicate, and it is not of the least consequence whether we call it an 'object' or an 'extension.' The important thing is to recognise its function and to know its place in the sentence.

It will be allowed by all competent judges that the foundation of composition lies in the sentence, that no one can compose well who cannot write a good sentence, and that no one can *consciously* write a good sentence who does not understand the principles that govern sentence structure. To the exposition and exemplification of these principles a large part of this book is devoted; accordingly a prominent place is assigned to synthesis, to the placement of qualifying adjuncts—a most difficult part of composition—and to the devices usually adopted to bring emphatic words into positions of emphasis and related words into proximity.

I have endeavoured so to present this part of the subject as to induce in the young student a critical attitude of mind—critical, that is, as to his choice of modes of expression and as to the merits or the defects of this or of that mode. In his excellent *Companion* to his *Higher English Grammar*, Professor Bain says: 'In teaching English the most effective course seems to me to be this: having selected an exemplary passage, first to assign its peculiar excellence and its deficiency, and next to point out what things contribute to the one and what to the other, and what are indifferent to both. *The pupils are thus accustomed to weigh every expression that comes before them, and this I take to be the beginning of the art of composition.*' The spirit of this passage and of Bain's teaching is the governing spirit of this little manual, which, however, does not pretend to go beyond the elements of composition. It deals with the structure of sentences of many forms and of several degrees of complexity, but not with the paragraph and the connectives that give movement to the paragraph and the larger divisions of the paragraph. For a full and masterly treatment of the whole subject the teacher is referred to Bain's books on English.

In connection with the pronoun and the complex sentence of two clauses I have introduced the subject of equivalent modes of expression. This part of composition is of great interest and importance, and is deserving of much fuller treatment than it has received in this book. For a very full and able treatment of it the teacher is referred to Mr. A. F. Murison's *First Work in English*, published, like Professor Bain's books, by Messrs. Longmans and Co.

The exemplary passages, and the passages for analysis and synthesis, are, with a few unimportant exceptions, selected by myself from our most idiomatic prose writers. They are, with one or two exceptions, selected from prose writings, for the obvious reason that prose composition can be taught only from prose models. The language of the examples and exercises, though not more difficult than that of the reading-books of the classes for which this book is intended, is yet sufficiently difficult to make the pupils respect it. It is my experience that many of the prose examples in most text-books of analysis are so unlike the sentences of the reading-books, so simple (not to say childish) that boys and girls of average ability despise them. They do not see what good can come from a study of them.

The analysed sentences furnish the pupils with a large

amount of good material for putting into practice the principles of composition expounded in the text. The synthesising of these examples should prove one of the most profitable as well as one of the most interesting exercises in the book. For the assistance and convenience of teachers a key to the synthesis is published separately.

Another very useful exercise is the correction of errors in grammar and arrangement. Examples of such errors are inserted here and there in the book. Some of these are of my own selecting, but most of them are taken from the fine collection of the late Dr. Hodgson, whose book, *Errors in the Use of English*, should be in the library of every teacher.

On every page of his pupils' reading-books, the teacher will find passages exemplifying some of the principles explained and exemplified in this book. Such passages should be used as supplementary exercises. Besides word-parsing for concord and government, the teacher should give his pupils a considerable amount of phrase- and clause-parsing for position. For this exercise the reading-books furnish abundance of fine material. It is a good exercise to set the pupils to search their reading lessons for examples of this or of that construction.

The reading-books also furnish examples of paragraph structure, of the elements of style, including figures of speech, and of the phrases and connectives that are usually employed to mark transitions of thought and to give movement to paragraphs and the larger divisions of the paragraph (see Bain's *Rhetoric and Composition*, Pt. I.) In the same books is to be found plenty of good material for exemplifying the difference between the diction of prose and that of poetry. It is unquestionable that, in the hands of a competent teacher, the reading-books can be made a most powerful instrument for teaching the essentials of good form in prose composition. Even their errors can be turned to account in teaching what to avoid.

'In composition, as in grammar, we need two courses of instruction, running side by side. The first is, a systematic course of principles, with appropriate examples; the second, a critical examination of texts, passages, or writings, as they occur in some of the good English authors. The two methods support and confirm each other, while either by itself is unsatisfactory. If there *are* principles of composition, they ought to be set forth in systematic array, and not left to irregular and random presentation. On the other hand, unless we grapple with some continuous text, we can neither find adequate exemplification, nor give any assurance of the completeness of our theories' (Bain, *On Teaching English*, p. 23).

In this little book I have attempted to supply 'a systematic course of principles, with appropriate examples'; the school reading-books supply the other essential— 'passages for critical examination.'

Suggestions for the improvement of the book and corrections of misprints and other errors will be gratefully received by the publishers or by myself.

To Mr. J. Wetherell, M.A., Head-master of Towcester Grammar School, who has kindly performed for me the disagreeable task of seeing the book through the press, I gladly tender my sincere thanks.

P. GOYEN.

CONTENTS

PART I

THE SIMPLE SENTENCE

	PAGE
1. Logical Analysis	1
2. Grammatical Analysis: Subject, Predicate, Object	2
3. Concord of Subject and Predicate	4
4. The Function of the Adjective	8
5. Kinds of Adjuncts to the Noun	10
6. Placement of Adjuncts to the Noun	11
7. Pronouns and Pronominal Couples	12
8. Adverbial Adjuncts	18
9. Placement of Adverbial Adjuncts	19
10. Order and Distribution of Adverbial Adjuncts	21
11. Usual Placement of Subject, Predicate, and Object	26
12. Departure from the usual Order for the sake of Emphasis and Energy	27
13. Analysis	28
14. Synthesis	28

PART II

THE COMPLEX SENTENCE OF TWO CLAUSES

1. The Noun Clause: its Place and its Equivalents	39
2. The Adjective (Relative) Clause and its Equivalents	43

	PAGE
3. The Adverbial Clause and its Equivalents	46
4. Interchange of Adverb with Adverbial Phrase	48
5. Placement of the Relative Clause	50
6. Note on the Relative Clause	54
7. Syntax of the Relative Pronouns	56
8. Placement of the Adverbial Clause	62
9. Note on 'Do' and 'So'	67
10. Note on the Comparisons	68
11. Analysis	70
12. Synthesis	73
13. An Important Participial Construction: its Place and its Equivalents	84
14. Absolute Phrases: their Place and their Equivalents	89

PART III

THE COMPOUND SENTENCE

1. The Copulative or Cumulative Relation	92
2. The Disjunctive Relation	93
3. The Compound Subordinate Clause	101
4. Mixed Sentences	106

PART IV

THE COMPLEX SENTENCE OF MORE THAN TWO CLAUSES

1. Analysis of Complex Sentences of more than two Clauses	109
2. Synthesis of Complex Sentences of more than two Clauses	112

PART I

THE SIMPLE SENTENCE

Logical Analysis

A SIMPLE sentence is a group of words by which:
  I. A statement is made, as:

 'Birds fly.' 'The fire burns.' 'The boy has learnt his lessons.'

  II. A question is asked, as:

 'Why do you run so fast?' 'Who bought these articles?'

  III. A command or a wish is expressed, as:

 'Go (thou).' 'Speak (you).' 'May you be happy.'

Every simple sentence contains at least two parts, the *subject* and the *predicate*. The *subject* is the word (or words) denoting the person about whom or the thing about which something is asserted. The *predicate* is the word (or words) by means of which something is asserted of the subject.

These parts, the subject and the predicate, are the essential parts of every sentence; all other parts of the sentence group themselves to the one or the other of these. Hence a sentence, however long, may be regarded as consisting only of subject and predicate.

A sentence broken up into these two parts is said to be analysed.

Examples

Subject.	Predicate.
Our old house	was vacant.
I	played some old tunes.
He	ordered his dinner.
This state of mind	could not last long.
A plain stone	was placed over his grave.
The state of the city	was becoming frightful.
The fighting men of the garrison	were much exhausted.
Several of them	fell down from exhaustion.

This is called the logical analysis of the sentences. In grammar we take note of more minute divisions of the sentence. These you will learn as you proceed.

Exercise I

1. Give the logical analysis of the following sentences:

Alfred was taught at home. He had a strong liking for books. His mother was a kind-hearted woman. The two lads grew up together. The noise was a false alarm. The poet spoke of his own songs. His health seemed to have mended. I shall not easily forget you. He lives eight miles from his post town. They retired into the library. The friends of that day were few in number.

2. Write down the logical analysis of ten sentences of your own construction.

3. Give the logical analysis of twenty sentences selected from your reading-book.

Grammatical Analysis: Subject, Predicate, Object

The *grammatical subject* may be:

    1. A noun, as: '*Birds* fly.'
    2. A pronoun, as: '*They* fly.'
    3. An adjective, as: '*The good* are happy.'

THE SIMPLE SENTENCE

    4. An infinitive, as: '*To lie* is disgraceful.'
    5. A verbal noun, as: '*Riding* is good exercise.'
    6. A sentence, as: 'I declare *you are wrong*.'

The *grammatical predicate* may be:

I. An **intransitive verb**, as:

    'Birds *fly*.'
    'The ship *sailed*.'
    'The child *cried*.'
    'Our friends *have departed*.'
    'The children *had been playing*.'

Notice here that, without the assistance of other words, each verb expresses complete sense. Such verbs are called *verbs of complete predication*.

II. The verbs '*be*,' '*seem*,' '*grow*,' '*appear*,' '*become*,' and some others, with an adjective, a noun, a pronoun, an adverb, or other words, as:

    1. 'The man *is (seems, appears, becomes) happy*.'
    2. 'These men *are giants*.'
    3. 'Mary *is here (there, yonder)*.'
    4. 'She *is of unsound mind*.'
    5. 'The verdict *was that he was guilty*.'

Observe that these verbs cannot, without the assistance of other words, express complete sense. They are therefore called *verbs of incomplete predication*. They are also called *copulative verbs*, because their function is to join the real predicate to the subject.

III. A **transitive verb**, as:

    'The wind *broke* the tree.'
    'James *struck* John.'

Transitive verbs also are *verbs of incomplete predication*; for, without an object, they are generally unable to express complete sense. Hence the object of a transitive verb is sometimes called the *completion of the predicate*. For the purposes of analysis it is called the *object* of the sentence. Like the subject, the object may be a noun, a pronoun, an adjective, an infinitive, a verbal noun (with or without qualifying words), and a noun sentence.

The *subject* of the sentence is said to be in the *nominative case*, and the *object* is said to be in the *objective case*.

Concord of Subject and Predicate

Rule.—*The subject and predicate (verb) must agree in number and person. Of whatever number and person the subject is, of the same number and person must the predicate (verb) be.*

Examples

1. 'The hounds chase the hare.'

The subject 'hounds' is plural and of the 3rd person.
The predicate 'chase' is plural and of the 3rd person.
Hence there is the proper agreement between the subject and the predicate of the sentence.

2. 'Some birds eats insects.'

The subject 'birds' is plural and of the 3rd person.
The predicate 'eats' is singular and of the 3rd person.
The subject and predicate, therefore, agree in person, but *not* in number. The sentence should be written : 'Some birds eat insects.'

Exercise II

1. Parse in the same way the subject and the predicate (verb) of each of the following sentences :

We continue our course. They discovers an island. He enters upon the scene. We enters upon the scene. You descried the eastern range. He give me a suitable present. We was all there together. The natives hit upon a mode of treatment. The two boys was fond of each other. Peacocks has long tails. The birds in the tree is singing. The children living at the end of this street goes to school. Nothing but dreary dykes occur to break the monotony of the landscape. The existence of these differences do not justify the quarrel. A sojourn of five years in the hospitals have strengthened these opinions. The loss of Wilkie and Chantrey seem not likely to be soon supplied. His knowledge of French and Italian literature were far beyond the common. Exactly opposite each other stands a church and a gin-palace.

2. Place a suitable subject to each of the following predicates : Sings, have sung, fly, has flown, shines, fall, springs,

blow, sparkles, has spoken, have spoken, hadst slept, singest, hast sung, hearest, hast heard.

3. Place a predicate to each of the following subjects : Fire, horses, water, stars, winds, snow, the cat, men, we, thou, he, they, you, I.

4. Write ten sentences consisting of subject, predicate, and object.

Rule.—*Two or more singular subjects connected by 'and' require a plural verb*, as :

(a) 'James and John have gone to town.'
(b) 'He and his sister are in the next room.'
(c) { 'He and I }
    { 'You and I } were the best of friends.'
(d) { 'Peter, James, and John were the chief apostles.'
    { 'Peter and James and John were the chief apostles.'

When there are more than two subjects the conjunction 'and' is sometimes omitted ; even with the omission of 'and,' however, the verb must be plural, as :

(a) 'Health, youth, beauty are the gifts of nature.'
(b) 'Pride, conscience, party spirit were on the side of the Tories.'

The omission of the conjunction adds energy to the sentence. Note that :

    James and John = they.
    He and his sister = they.
    He and I   = we.
    You and I = we.
    They and I = we.
    You and they = you.

Exercise III

Correct the following and give reasons for the changes you make :

John and I was present. Quietness and peace is to be had here. Scott and Dickens has written excellent novels. The duke and his servants has just departed. She and I has just arrived. Diligence and industry counts for more than talent. Where justice and reason governs, there peace and happiness flourishes. My sister and I am going to see the play. Faith and hope is in their prime. Honour, justice, religion was involved.

Rule.—*Two or more singular subjects connected by 'or,' 'nor,' 'either,' 'neither,' require a singular verb,* as :

(a)
- 'My sister or my brother has written to you.'
- 'Either my sister or my brother has written to you.'
- 'James, his sister, or his brother has written to you.'
- 'Either James, or his sister, or his brother has written to you.'

Note the repetition of 'or' in the last sentence.

(b) 'Neither James nor John is willing to go.'
(c) 'Neither wind, nor rain, nor anything else is able to cool our affections.'

Note the repetition of 'nor' in the last sentence.

Rule.—*If one of the subjects connected by these conjunctions is plural the verb must be plural, and the plural subject should be placed next to the verb,* as :

(a) 'Either John or his sisters have called to see you.'
(b) 'Neither John nor his sisters have called to see you.'

Rule.—*When two or more pronouns of different persons are used as subjects and connected by 'or' or 'nor,' the verb should agree with the pronoun next to it,* as :

(a) 'Neither he nor I am at fault.'
(b) 'Neither I nor he is at fault.'
(c) 'Either you or he is at fault.'
(d) 'Either he or you are at fault.'

This arrangement has the sanction of good authority. It is, however, a very awkward one, and should be avoided except in cases in which the verb has the same form for the persons and numbers of the pronouns used, as :

(a) 'Neither $\begin{Bmatrix} \text{he nor I} \\ \text{I nor he} \end{Bmatrix}$ can be at fault.'

(b) 'Either $\begin{Bmatrix} \text{you or he} \\ \text{he or you} \end{Bmatrix}$ must be at fault.'

When each of the pronouns requires a different form of the verb, the following construction should be adopted :

(a) 'He is not at fault, nor am I.'
(b) 'I am not at fault, nor is he.'
(c) 'Either you are at fault, or he is.'
(d) 'Either he is at fault, or you are.'

Rule.—*Two singular nouns connected by 'as well as' require a singular verb,* as :

(a) 'Cæsar, as well as Cicero, was a great man.'

(b) 'The tone of the act, as well as the substance of it, indicates the direction in which the tide was setting.'

'As well as' indicates comparison, not combination.

Rule.—*Subjects individualised by the distributive adjectives,* '*each*,' '*every*,' '*either*,' '*neither*,' *require a singular verb and a singular pronoun,* as :

(a) '*Each* of the men *works* in *his* own way.'
(b) '*Each* of us *knows* best where *his* own difficulties lie.'
(c) 'Meantime the two brothers were *each* wrapped up in *his* own reflections.'
(d) '*Each* party *tries* to serve those for whom *it is* interested ; but *neither* party *consents* to grant favourable terms to *its* enemies.'
(e) '*Every* man and *every* nation *has its* own characteristic vices.'
(f) '*Every* smith, *every* carpenter, *every* cutler *was* at constant work on the guns and blades assigned to *him*.'

'Many a' is joined to a singular subject, as :

(a) '*Many a* flower *is* born to blush unseen.'
(b) 'So inviting was the conception that *many an* English adventurer *was* willing to try *his* hand to convert it into reality.'

The following constructions should be noted :

(a) 'Fort after fort *was* taken.'
(b) 'Noble after noble *was* hurried to the block.'
(c) 'Fitzgerald with his uncles *was* committed to the Tower.'
(d) 'The young lord with three of his uncles *was* on the spot by daybreak.'
(e) 'Much beef, brandy, and harness *was* found in the magazines' (= much of beef, etc.)

'*None*' means 'not one,' or 'no one,' and ought, therefore, to take a singular verb. Even the best writers, however, assign to it sometimes a singular and sometimes a plural verb.

EXAMPLES

(a) '*None* but members of the Church of Rome *were* thought worthy of any mark of royal favour' (Macaulay).
(b) '*None* of the modes by which a magistrate is appointed *affords* much security for his being wiser than any of his neighbours' (Macaulay).
(c) '*None* of them *was* deficient in abilities, and four of them were men of high intellectual eminence' (Macaulay).

Exercise IV

Correct the following, and give reasons for the changes you make:

Either my brother or my sister are willing to do the work. His peace or his fortune are at stake. Neither the lawyer nor the judge were able to understand the case. James, as well as John, have taken a good position in their class. Neither you nor I are to blame. Either I or you am to blame. The king or his ministers is to be present at the ceremony. Each of them owe a debt of gratitude to their deliverer. Every sailor and every soldier are expected to do their duty. Venus, as well as the earth, revolve round the sun. Neither of your plans satisfy me. Neither of the chief authorities appear to have participated in the general feeling. The gain to the French seem not to have been great. One of his papers were found in the box. Homer as well as Virgil were studied on the banks of the Rhine. Are neither of these your friend? Ten months' interest are due. Too great a variety of studies distract the mind. Fortress after fortress were taken. James with his sister were at the play. Concession after concession were made in this way. More than one principle has been contended for at one time (more than one = at least two principles). Much butter, sugar, and salt were sold. The two great parties of the Christian world have each their own standard of truth. Each of these topics need a lecture for their development. Catholic communities have, since that time, become infidel and become Catholic again; but none have become Protestant.

The Function of the Adjective

Nouns, whatever position in the sentence they occupy, may have adjectives, or words equivalent to adjectives, attached to them.

Examples

(a) 'Horses draw loads.'
(b) 'Our horses draw your loads.'
(c) 'Our draught horses draw your heavy loads.'
(d) 'Our black draught horses draw your heavy loads of wood.'

The subject and the object of (b), (c), and (d) are said to be *qualified*, *limited*, or *enlarged*; and the qualifying words are sometimes called *enlargements*. They are so called, not because they make the sentence larger, but because they specify the attributes, qualities, or relations possessed by the things denoted by the nouns to which they are joined, and in this way *enlarge our knowledge* of the things.

In (*a*) all horses that draw loads and all loads that are drawn by horses are included. The terms 'horses' and 'loads,' therefore, include a large number of individuals.

In (*b*) are included only the horses that belong to us and the loads that belong to you; all other horses and loads are (by implication) excluded. Hence fewer individuals are denoted by the nouns in (*b*) than by the same nouns in (*a*).

In (*c*) are included only the draught horses that belong to us and the heavy loads that belong to you; all our other horses and all your other loads are (by implication) excluded. Fewer individuals are, therefore, denoted by the nouns in (*c*) than by the same nouns in (*b*), and therefore than by the same nouns in (*a*); and it is obvious that still fewer are denoted by the same nouns in (*d*), for this sentence excludes all our draught horses that are not black and all your heavy loads that do not consist of wood.

And always, as the qualifying words are increased, the number of individuals denoted by the noun to which the qualifying words are added is decreased. *Each qualifying word adds to the meaning of the noun, but narrows its range or limits its application.*

'*Adjuncts*' means something added: all words added to nouns to define their meaning in the sentence we shall call *qualifying adjuncts*, or *limiting adjuncts*.

Some adjuncts specify quantity only, as:

(*a*) 'Some things.'   'Much sugar.'
(*b*) 'Ten men.'   'Twenty pounds.'

Such adjuncts limit the quantity of the thing, or the number of things, denoted by the noun.

In (*a*) the limitation is indefinite, or inexact.

In (*b*) the limitation is definite, or exact.

Note.—The adjective as predicate does not limit; it simply specifies a quality of the subject.

KINDS OF ADJUNCTS TO NOUNS

Qualifying or limiting adjuncts to the noun may consist of:
(*a*) Adjectives (examples have been given).
(*b*) A preposition with a noun, as:

1. 'The pleasures *of the country*.'
2. 'A glance *at a map*.'
3. 'A space *in the centre of a large city*.'
4. 'The whole period *between October and March*.'
5. 'A present *for James*.'
6. 'A present *from his father*.'
7. 'A boy *with curly hair*.'
8. 'Courtesy *towards our companions*.'
9. 'The road *along the shore*.'
10. 'The bird's right *to life and freedom*.'
11. 'The food *on the table*.'
12. 'The bird *in the cage*.'

Such phrases are called *prepositional phrases*.

(*c*) A noun or a pronoun in the possessive case, as:

'The *boy's* hat.'   '*John's* brother.'   '*Their* home.'
'*My* lessons.'   '*His* book.'

(*d*) A noun in apposition, as:

(1) 'John, *the fisherman*.'   (2) 'Cromwell, *the Protector*.'

(*e*) A verb in the infinitive mood, as:

(1) 'A house *to let*.'   (2) 'Bread *to eat*.'
(3) 'Water *to drink*.'   (4) 'Lessons *to be learnt*.'

The participial adjunct we shall deal with later on.

EXERCISE V

1. From the following sentences select the qualifying or limiting adjuncts, and state of what they consist and what they qualify or limit:

Inner sunshine warms the heart. There was no time for smiles. There was mighty work to be done. Amid the grinding tear of the shot through the rigging, the sailors did noble duty. He made many important improvements in machinery. The woods showed all the colours of the rainbow. Puss had no great zeal for the fine arts. The village in the valley was swept away. Obedience is the key to every door. The difference between the brothers was great. Slight drizzling showers were falling. This part of Africa was the scene of Livingstone's labours. In the fold on the hill there are twenty fat sheep. Puss is the only other article to be considered here. Mary, Queen of Scots, was executed in the reign of Elizabeth. Mr. Gladstone, the great English statesman, is a man of wonderful ability. There was water everywhere, but not a drop to drink. The thunder from the guns on the right showed that the English were gaining a mastery over the enemy. The tricks to be performed to-night are very amusing. Walpole had eminent talents for government and debate.

2. Add as many limiting adjuncts as you can to the following nouns: Sugar, plain, elephant, paper, cracks, oysters, prisoner, hat, soldiers, wine, nation, thief, servants.

Place of Adjuncts to the Noun

The general rule is: *That qualifying adjuncts must be placed as near as possible to what they are intended to qualify.* This position is either immediately before or immediately after the word intended to be qualified.

Read again the sentences in the last exercise, and observe that the adjective and the possessive case *precede*, and that the noun in apposition, the prepositional phrase, and the infinitive *follow* the noun to which they are adjuncts. In prose this is their usual placement.

The adjective as predicate usually follows the subject, as:

    (*a*) 'The answer was *short*, *clear*, and *decisive*.'
    (*b*) 'The natives of wine-countries are generally *sober*.'

Two or more adjectives of quality sometimes follow the noun to which they are adjuncts, as:

    (*a*) 'All their disputes, *internal and external*, were decided by foreign influence.'
    (*b*) 'The native troops, *regular and irregular*, broke away.'

An adjective qualified by a phrase is generally placed after the noun to which it is an adjunct, as:

    (*a*) 'Laws *hostile to the people* were passed by the parliament.'
    (*b*) 'The historians *the most partial to the minister* admit the truth of these stories.'

To sum up we may say that, as a rule, *short simple adjuncts precede and long complex adjuncts follow the noun.*

Exercise VI

Parse the phrasal limiting adjuncts contained in one or more of your reading lessons.

Note.—The prepositional phrase is the chief phrasal adjunct.

Pronouns and Pronominal Couples

The demonstrative pronouns '*he,*' '*she,*' '*it,*' '*they,*' like the relative pronouns '*who,*' '*which,*' '*that,*' all look backward, and the function of each of them is to represent an *antecedent noun with all its limiting adjuncts*. With this noun (called its *antecedent* or *subject of reference*) the pronoun must agree in *number*, *person*, and *gender*. These little words, simple as they look, are very troublesome to manage, and the young student cannot be too careful in his use of them. He must be especially careful to see:

1. *That the pronoun has a subject of reference, and that the subject is sufficiently prominent and sufficiently near to the pronoun to make the reference easy to the reader.*

2. *That there are not two or more different subjects to any one of which the pronoun may reasonably be referred.* (This is a fruitful source of error.)

The following examples, selected from the works of experienced writers, show how easy it is to misuse the demonstrative pronouns:

(*a*) 'No one as yet had exhibited the structure of the human kidneys, Vesalius having only examined *them* in dogs.'

The antecedent of 'them' is, not 'kidneys,' but 'human kidneys'; hence the writer represents Vesalius as having examined *human kidneys* in dogs!

(*b*) 'The pedant assured his (1) patron that although he (2) could not divest the boy of the knowledge he (3) had already imbibed, unless he (4) would empower him (5) to disable his (6) fingers, he (7) should endeavour, with God's help, to prevent his (8) future improvement.'

Here his (1), he (2), him (5), he (7) refer to pedant; he (3), his (6), and his (8) refer to boy; and he (4) refers to patron. This cross-fire of pronouns is most perplexing.

(c) 'In Spain *freedom* of thought, or, at least, the *free* expression of *it*, has been so closely fettered, that science in its strictest sense has made little progress in that unhappy country.'

'It' ought to be referred to 'freedom of thought,' the most prominent subject of reference in the antecedent phrase; the writer does not, however, intend the pronoun to refer to the principal noun 'freedom,' but to the subordinate noun 'thought'; he should, therefore, have written: 'In Spain freedom of thought, or, at least, the free expression of thought,' etc. *In all cases it is better to repeat the noun than to cause obscurity by the misuse of the pronoun.*

(d) '*Her* own story was that *she* had a quarrel with the deceased, first about *her* wages, and secondly about the soup, and that *she* seized the deceased by the throat, and *she* fell, and when *she* got up *she* was looking for something to strike *her* with, and upon this *she* struck the deceased a blow on the throat, and *she* fell, and died almost instantaneously.'

I leave, as a puzzle for the pupil, the discovery of the subjects of reference in this and the next example:

(e) 'Two other words occur to me which are very commonly mangled by our clergy. One of these is "covetous" and its substantive "covetousness." I hope some who read these lines will be induced to leave off pronouncing *them* "covetious" and "covetiousness." I can assure *them* that when *they* do thus call *them*, one, at least, of *their* hearers has his appreciation of *their* teaching disturbed.'

(f) 'My resolution is to spare no expense on education; *it* is a bad calculation, because *it* is the only advantage over which circumstances have no power.'

The first 'it' has no subject of reference, and some thought is required to determine the subject of the second 'it.' The meaning intended is: 'The *sparing of expense* on education is a bad calculation, because education is the only,' etc.

(g) 'A statute inflicting death may be, and ought to be, repealed, if *it* be in any degree expedient.'

'It' ought to be referred to 'a statute inflicting death.' This, however, would make nonsense. The author intended 'it' to refer to a subject implied in the predicate of the antecedent sentence, viz. 'the repeal,' 'such repeal,' 'the repeal of such a statute.' In this sentence the *implied reference* gives too much trouble to the reader. In the following the implied reference is, in each case, easy and therefore allowable.

(*h*) 'He expected to be condemned to death; he even desired *it*' (it=to be condemned to death).

(*i*) 'He broke the rules and was punished for *it*' (it=breaking the rules).

The pronoun 'it' often has a forward or anticipative reference, as:

'*It* is good that I was afflicted,' *where* 'it' *represents* 'that I was afflicted.'

THIS AND THAT AS PRONOUNS

EXAMPLES

(*a*) '*This* is good, but *that* is better.'

When 'this' and 'that' are so used, 'this' refers to the nearer and 'that' to the more remote thing spoken of. Their plural forms *these* and *those* are used in the same way, as:

'*These* are yours and *those* are mine.'

(*b*) 'Some place the bliss in action, some in ease, *Those* call it pleasure, and contentment *these*.'

'Those' refers to the more remote 'some,' the people that place the bliss in action; 'these' refers to the nearer 'some,' the people that place the bliss in ease.

In prose other *pronominal couples*, as they are called, might be substituted for 'those' and 'these,' as:

1. '*The former* find their pleasure in action, and *the latter* theirs in ease.'
2. '*The first* find their pleasure in action, and *the second* (or *the last*) theirs in ease.'

(*c*) 'Virtue and vice are before you; *this* leads to misery, *that* to peace' (this=vice, that=virtue).

VARIATIONS OF (*c*)

1. 'Virtue and vice are before you; *the one* (=the first named, virtue) leads to peace, *the other* (=vice) to misery.'
2. 'Virtue and vice are before you; *the former* leads to peace, *the latter* to misery.'
3. 'Virtue and vice are before you; *the first* leads to peace, *the second* (or *the last*) to misery.'

THE SIMPLE SENTENCE

(*d*) 'Both international and municipal law were in favour of Charles; he was a prisoner of war by *the former*, a king by *the latter*' ('the former' = international law, 'the latter' = municipal law).

VARIATIONS OF (*d*)

1. '... he was a prisoner of war by *the one*, a king by *the other*.'
2. '... he was a prisoner of war by *that*, a king by *this*.'
3. '... he was a prisoner of war by *the first*, a king by *the second* (or *the last*).'

'That' with its plural 'those' followed by 'of' is often substituted for a noun: '*that of*,' '*those of*.'

EXAMPLES

(*a*) 'The influence of Becket rivalled the influence of the king.'
= The influence of Becket rivalled *that* of the king.
= Becket's influence rivalled the king's.
(*b*) 'The poetry of Milton differs from the poetry of Dante.'
= The poetry of Milton differs from *that* of Dante.
= Milton's poetry differs from Dante's.
(*c*) 'The preface is the preface of a man firm in his own religious opinions and tolerant towards the religious opinions of others.'
= The preface is *that* of a man firm in his own religious opinions and tolerant towards *those* of others (those = not opinions, but religious opinions).

Before writing 'that' or 'those' in this construction, mentally substitute the noun (or the noun with its adjunct) for which it is intended to stand; if you cannot do so readily, do not use the pronoun. Had the writer of the following sentence tried this mental substitution of the noun for the pronoun, he would have adopted another construction:

'Another mode of spending the leisure time is *that* of books.'

The only possible subject of reference is 'mode'; substituting 'mode' for '*that*' we have:

'Another mode of spending the leisure time is the mode of books,' which is nonsense.

The following sentence exemplifies three of the foregoing constructions:

'Every kind of affectation is to be found on the other side of the Channel—*the soldier's* and *the sportsman's, that of* the dandy and *that of* the man who is "used up," *the affectation of fashion* and *the affectation of Liberty Hall*.'

ONE as a Pronoun
Examples

(a) '*One* should control *one's* feelings.'

Be careful not to write:

'*One* should control *his* feelings.'

(b) 'These are trifles that *one* gets used to, and in fact *one* would hardly think *oneself* in the tropics without them.'

Anticipatory Use of Pronouns
Examples

(a) 'As soon as they had finished their repast, the young people rose from the table.'

Here 'they' looks forward to 'young people.'
The usual construction is:

'As soon as the young people had finished their repast, they rose from the table.'

(b) 'When he saw his error, the boy at once corrected it.'
= When the boy saw his error, he at once corrected it.

Exercise VII

1. Refer to their antecedents the demonstrative pronouns used in one or more of your reading lessons.

2. Point out the faults of pronominal reference in the following:

(1) Metissa brought with her an old maid recommended by her mother, who taught *her* all the arts of domestic management. *They* soon invented one reason or another to quarrel with all my servants, and either prevailed on me to turn *them* away or treated *them* so ill that *they* left me of *themselves*, and *they* always supplied *their* places with some brought from my wife's family.

(2) Adversity gives wisdom; *it* ought to be greatly prized.

(3) The wind blew down the wall; *it* was very high.

(4) The Emperor Alexander presented to the Emperor William a portrait of *himself*.

(5) He allowed his brother to take his place for a short time, and for that short time *he* was a constant source of annoyance.

(6) Mr. A. presents his compliments to Mr. B. *I* have got a

hat which is not *his;* if *he* have got a hat which is not *yours,* no doubt *they* are the missing ones.

(7) The lad cannot leave his father, for if he should leave him *he* would die.

(8) And it came to pass that night that the angel of the Lord went out and smote in the camp of the Assyrians one hundred fourscore and five thousand ; and, when *they* arose early in the morning, behold *they* were all dead corpses.

(9) At the lower end of the hall is a large otter's skin stuffed with hay, which Sir Roger's mother ordered to be hung up in that manner, and the knight looks upon *it* with great satisfaction, because *it* seems he was but nine years old when *his* dog killed *him.*

(10) The grand jury found true bills against the agitators ; and, although *they* threw every obstacle in the way of the proceedings, *they* were successfully carried through.

3. Substitute other pronominal couples for those used in the following sentences :

It is open to us to fight or to retreat ; *this* is a disgrace, *that* is madness. Two treaties were drawn up ; one on white paper, the other on red, the *former* real, the *latter* fictitious. I have always preferred cheerfulness to mirth ; *the one* I consider as an act, *the other* as a habit of the mind. I admit discussion on every matter except dinner and debts ; I hold that *the first* must be eaten and *the second* must be paid. He knew both Francis and Hastings ; *the former* he mistrusted, *the latter* he hated. I will not barter English commerce for Irish slavery ; *that* is not the price I would pay, nor is *this* the thing I would purchase.

4. In each of the following sentences substitute the noun for the pronoun **that** or **those** :

His claim was no better founded than *that* of Catherine or *that* of the Bonaparte family in Spain. The style of Frances bears a strong resemblance to *that* of Junius. It was safer to take the part of Hastings in a minority than *that* of Francis in a majority. The poems of Tennyson are more widely read than *those* of Wordsworth. The manners of the Britons differed from *those* of the Romans. The men and the horses were more powerful than *those* of the Carnatic. Sir John Malcolm compares the conduct of Clive with *that* of the Duke of Wellington. His power far surpassed *that* which Dupleix had attained.

5. Write the following sentences in as many equivalent forms as you can:

The eloquence of Cicero was superior to the eloquence of Cæsar. The poems of Dryden differ from the poems of Tennyson. The conduct of Hastings was more manly than the conduct of his rival. The writings of Macaulay are more brilliant than the writings of Alison. Less is known of the life of Shakespeare than of the life of Milton. The conduct of Impey was more disgraceful than the conduct of Hastings. The influence of the king outweighed the influence of his minister. The light of the sun is more brilliant than the light of the moon. The career of Wellington was more honourable than the career of Napoleon.

ADVERBIAL ADJUNCTS

The assertion made by the predicate is generally qualified by circumstances of **time**, of **place**, of **manner**, or of **cause**. The words added to the predicate to specify these circumstances are called *qualifying*, or *limiting*, or *modifying* adjuncts to the predicate. They are also called *extensions* of the predicate. These adjuncts consist more frequently of prepositional phrases than of single words, and no small part of the art of composition lies in the setting of such phrases in the sentence.

I. Adjuncts of Time

(a) 'My father came *yesterday*.' } Point of time.
(b) 'I started *at sunrise*.'
(c) 'The lecture lasted *three hours*.' } Duration of time.
(d) 'I was present *during the whole day*.'
(e) 'The postman comes *twice a day*.' Repetition of time.

II. Adjuncts of Place

(a) 'He was born *in London*.' } Rest in a place.
(b) 'He remains *there*.'
(c) 'We are bound *for England*.' Motion to a place.
(d) 'We are returning *from America*.' Motion from a place.

III. ADJUNCTS OF MANNER

(a) 'Some birds fly *quickly*.'   Manner strictly.
(b) 'The army was *quite* exhausted.'   Degree.
(c) 'He cut the apple *with his knife*.'   Instrument.
(d) 'He was ruined *by a friend*.'   Agent.
(e) 'I performed the journey *with my brother*.'   { Accompanying circumstances.

IV. ADJUNCTS OF CAUSE

(a) 'We eat *to live*.'
(b) 'He acted *from prejudice*.'   } Motive, ground, reason.
(c) '*With industry* he will succeed.'   Condition.
(d) 'The ear was made *for hearing*.'   Purpose.

Causal adjuncts express many shades of meaning that are very difficult to classify. Adverbs, it may be added, are used to modify adjectives and other adverbs.

RULES FOR PLACE OF THE ADVERBIAL ADJUNCT

The simple adverb is placed:—

I. Before the adjective or the adverb it is intended to qualify, as:

(a) 'The girl is *extremely* unhappy.'
(b) 'The speaker spoke *very* rapidly.'

II. Between the auxiliary and the participle, as:

(a) 'He had *long* considered his life a burden.'
(b) 'In this battle the king was *completely* vanquished.'
(c) 'His plan should be *greatly* modified.'

III. Between the auxiliary and the active infinitive, as:

(a) 'We should *never* speak ill of the dead.'
(b) 'You should *gently* reprove him for his fault.'

IV. Sometimes before and sometimes after the simple verb, as:

(a) 'The king *openly* opposed the proposal.'
(b) 'The king opposed the proposal *openly*.'
(c) 'He *savagely* flung himself upon his enemy.'
(d) 'He flung himself *savagely* upon his enemy.'

Rule I. is almost constant, but Rules II. and III. are frequently departed from. With respect to all qualifying words the general rule is **to place them so as to make it impossible to doubt as to what word or words they are intended to affect**; and in applying this rule it is necessary to bear constantly in mind the general principle that, in English, *qualifying words look* **forwards** *rather than* **backwards**.

EXAMPLES

(a) 'The new party expected *greatly* to influence politics.'
(b) 'The new party *greatly* expected to influence politics.'

In each of these cases the adverb 'greatly' affects only the words that follow it.

The remark that 'qualifying words look *forwards* rather than *backwards*' applies especially to **only, merely, not,** and some other single-word adverbs.

EXAMPLES OF **ONLY, MERELY, NOT**

(a) 'We are determined to move only in the beaten path.' ('Only' here affects 'in the beaten path.')
(b) 'We are determined only to move in the beaten path.' ('Only' here affects 'to move in the beaten path.')
(c) 'We are only determined to move in the beaten path.' ('Only' here affects 'determined to move,' etc. 'We are nothing but determined,' etc.)

Placed between a noun (or a pronoun) and a compound verb, or after a noun (or a pronoun) at the end of the sentence, **only** should be referred to the noun or the pronoun immediately preceding it, as:

1. 'We only are determined to move in the beaten path.' (Only we, no others. Here 'only' does the work of an adjective. 'We alone are,' etc.)

If we write: 'We only determined to move,' etc., then 'only' bears on 'determined,' etc. 'Only' seems unable to operate across an auxiliary verb.

2. 'We are determined to move in the beaten path only.' ('Only' should here be referred to 'beaten path,' and is equivalent to an adjective.)

If 'only' is intended to qualify a clause, it should be placed at the head of it, as:

ADVERBIAL ADJUNCTS

(d) 'Work is done well only when it is done seriously.'
(e) 'A peasant would kill a cow merely to get a pair of brogues.' ('Merely' bears on 'to get,' etc.)
(f) 'William showed that he was determined not to allow others to get the better of him.' ('Not' bears on 'to allow,' etc.)

Try 'merely' and 'not' in other situations, and observe the effect of their placement.

Exercise VIII

In the following sentences the adverbs 'only,' 'merely,' 'even,' 'not,' are so placed as not to express the meaning of the writers.

1. Say what is the meaning of each sentence as it stands.
2. So place these adverbs as to express what you consider to be the meaning intended by the writers:

The walrus only lived a few days. The muscle has only contracted for an instant. This is a question that we can only settle by experiment. Our history only afforded one precedent which was at all in point. The internal government of England could only be carried on by the advice of English ministers. This kind of work only shows the externals of the fashionable world. In this way success can only be achieved in a limited degree. I merely came to inform you of the fact. There was even no ditch before the gates of the city. Some zealous Whigs were unwilling even to grant this indulgence. Fools and fanatics only believe that they cannot be mistaken. Opportunity only exists for us so far as we are able to make use of it. The queen was not entreated to deceive herself. The commander had only yielded when to persist would have exposed the unfortunate city once more to sack and butchery.

Order and Distribution of Adverbial Adjuncts

. When two or more adverbial adjuncts are used in the same sentence, great care should be exercised in placing them, for upon their placement will depend, in no small degree, the clearness and poise of the sentence.

As a **general rule,** *adverbial adjuncts of time precede those of place, and those of place precede those of manner and of cause.*

EXAMPLES

(a) '*In the following September* the king was murdered *in Berkeley Castle.*' (Time phrase at the beginning and place phrase at the end of the sentence.)
(b) '*At the opening of the battle* the English archers were thrown *forward* to *rake the Scottish squares.*' (Time phrase at the beginning and place adverb and purpose phrase at the end of the sentence.)
(c) '*In the English fleet* disease had appeared *in a deadly form.*' (Place phrase at the beginning and manner phrase at the end of the sentence.)
(d) '*For the first time* the king had been opposed *by some of the peers.*' (Time phrase at the beginning and agency phrase at the end of the sentence.)

This order is, however, frequently departed from. 'The mere fact that the adverbial qualifications of a sentence are numerous is a sufficient reason for placing at the commencement the one that most sweepingly qualifies the whole sentence' (Bain). Hence the position of an adverbial adjunct is fixed partly by its importance; and its importance is determined partly by its length. The fact, too, that *the beginning and the end of the sentence are the positions of greatest emphasis* has much to do with the placing of emphatic words and phrases. *For emphatic adverbial adjuncts the head of the sentence is usually the position of greatest emphasis.*

EXAMPLES

(a) '*To avoid every appearance of pressure from England*, these conditions were *first* laid *before the Scotch Parliament.*'
(b) '*In spite of all their efforts to hold the post*, our men were driven *from it with the loss of half their number.*'

In each sentence there are three adverbial adjuncts, and in each the most important adjunct is placed at the head of the sentence, that is, where it can most 'sweepingly qualify the whole sentence.'

Without other change, place at the end of each sentence the adjunct now at its head, and observe how the sentence is weakened and how the sense 'draggles.' As each sentence now stands the sense is *suspended* until the end is reached. The writer has observed what is known as the **principle of suspense.** This is a principle of great importance in composition.

'Write your sentence in such a way that, until he has come to the full stop, the reader may feel the sentence to be incomplete' (Abbott).

As a rule, a sentence should not end with an unimportant word or phrase; hence, if two adverbial adjuncts are placed after the predicate, the shorter should generally precede the longer, as:

(a) 'They forced their way *successfully through the dangerous pass*.'
(b) 'The king looked *with pleasure on these hideous spectacles*.'

Invert the order of the adjuncts and note the effect.

When the object of a verb is loaded with adjuncts, a short adverbial phrase is properly placed between it and the verb, as:

(a) 'Such a defeat would now carry *with it* the resignation of the ministry.'
(b) 'The members had *in their minds* all their former serious grievances.'
(c) 'The people were ready to place *at the mercy of their sovereign* all their most ancient and precious rights.'

Exercise IX

1. Pick out and classify the adverbial adjuncts contained in one or more of your reading lessons, and note the position each occupies with respect to the word or words it qualifies.

2. Re-write the following sentences, placing the adverbial adjuncts according to the general rules given above:
The general acted with vigour at last. The supplies fell into the hands of the enemy in a few days. The wretched army marched out of the cantonments at length with much confusion. The army entered the defiles in bitter cold snow and without proper clothing. His bolder counsel prevailed after long and stormy discussion, and almost in spite of the general's wish. They forced their way successfully through the dangerous pass on the 16th of April. Matters continued in a dangerous state for many years. The king had the great council of the nobles around him. I had often received an invitation from my friend Sir Roger to pass away a month with him in the country. Johnson had received an uncouth figure and an irritable temper from nature. He would carry a sick and starving girl home on his shoulders from the streets. Johnson

was in the habit of sifting the evidence for all such stories with extreme severity. He could discern the folly and meanness of all bigotry except his own clearly enough. Sydney received a strange communication from him a short time after his disappearance. The English had forced their way into Connaught in a few minutes with the loss of twelve men. They took another matter of high importance into consideration on the same day. The traveller listens for the bark of a dog or the bleat of a lamb mile after mile in vain. William proceeded to the Hague after reposing some hours in the hut of a peasant. The exile had set foot again on his native soil after passing two years in a strange land. He became a classical master in a school after leaving Eton. We ought to place ourselves in our fathers' situation in order to form a correct estimate of their merits. The English people could not be long in recovering from the intoxication of loyalty under the government of such a man.

ANALYSIS OF SENTENCES

EXAMPLE

Analyse: 'To check this influence the representatives of the Liberals yearly produced a motion in favour of ballot at elections.'

Subject.	Limiting Adjuncts to Subject.	Predicate.	Object.	Limiting Adjuncts to Object.	Limiting Adjuncts to Predicate.
Representatives	1. the 2. of the Liberals	produced	motion	1. a 2. in favour of ballot at elections	to check this influence (purpose) yearly (time).

EXERCISE X

Analyse the following sentences, and note with great care the placement of the qualifying adjuncts:

Henceforward the Queen could repose her confidence in the

leader of either party. Ever since 1836 the trade of the country had been depressed. Warning is the principal end of punishment. To remove the offender is often one of the ends. To admire the book is to admire the author. To be a gentleman does not depend upon the tailor. The little child in the cradle slumbered peacefully. No thought of trouble entered the minds of the birds. To approach the well was almost certain death. He instantly gave the signal to start. He gave the signal to start instantly. The general feeling in favour of affording assistance in some shape was very strong. In the towns other general causes of suffering were at work. In the House the feeling in favour of continuing the work was represented by the Radicals. None the less did the leaders find in the new arrangements a ready means of exciting the anger of the people. In the competition for the trade the hand-worker was driven to ruin. With the want of an abundant supply of work wages began to fall. In nearly every manufacturing town trades unions made their appearance. At a time of depression of trade these unions offered a fresh difficulty to the employment of capital. In December 1837 Lord Brougham suggested a plan for national education. For the supply of teachers a normal school was to be established. The indignant clergy at first refused to accept any share of the grant. In the summer of 1838 the discontent began to assume dangerous proportions. The rejection of the petition was followed by a still worse riot. The revenue had been largely decreased by the somewhat reckless adoption of a very excellent reform. In spite of the threatened diminution of revenue the government boldly determined to risk the change. At such a range the artillery of that period could produce no important result upon the strong masonry of the forts. To secure Balaclava Sir Colin Campbell was stationed there with the Highland regiment. General Scarlett charged with his three hundred horsemen full in the face of the massive column. With perfect and unswerving gallantry Lord Cardigan galloped against the guns. The effort was from the first entirely a hopeless one. During many months the trade with the Mediterranean Sea had been almost entirely interrupted by the war. From the field of battle the king made his way through the multitude of fugitives to the neighbourhood of Louvain. Plots against the lives of obnoxious persons ever throve in the soil of the Scottish nature. From one point of view the attack upon Inkerman had been successful. This officer had ransacked the Mediterranean to procure wood to build huts for his troops. The misfortunes of the Crimean winter had produced a most powerful effect upon the English mind. On the 12th of December, at an unusually early time, Parliament was again assembled to enable ministers to bring in measures for the further continuation of the war. For the instant the nation was satisfied with the change. Under Miss Nightingale the defective arrangements for nursing had been rapidly improved. The concerted plan was ruined by an unfortunate error of one of the French generals. For some time hostility to the English had been visible at the Persian court. No coloured man was allowed under any circumstance to command Europeans. What does a man learn by travelling? The real use of travelling to distant countries and of studying the annals of past time is to preserve men from contraction of mind.

Exercise XI

Correct the following, and give reasons for your corrections:
One of the men sustained a wound in the arm of no importance. A piano for sale by a lady about to cross the Channel in an oak case with carved legs. The man blew out his brains after-bidding his wife good-bye with a gun. The Moor seizing a bolster, full of rage and jealousy, smothers his wife. Paid to a woman whose husband was drowned by order of the vestry under London Bridge, £1 : 1s. Erected to the memory of John Phillips accidentally shot as a mark of affection by his brother. People ceased to wonder by degrees. Perry saw a red flag hoisted in the harbour with a smile of contempt. The House affirmed the proposal to abolish university tests with enthusiasm. The Board of Education has resolved to erect a building large enough to accommodate five hundred students three stories high. I earnestly pressed his coming to us in my letter. They followed the advance of the party, step by step, through telescopes.

The Place of the Subject, the Predicate, and the Object

In prose the subject is usually placed before the predicate, and the predicate before the object; but, as words placed in

ANALYSIS OF SENTENCES

unusual positions gain emphasis thereby, this order is, either for the sake of emphasis and vigour or for the purpose of bringing related words into proximity, sometimes departed from.

Departure from the usual order for the sake of emphasis and vigour.

I. Adjective and noun predicate first:

(a) '*Wide* is the gate and *broad* is the way.'
(b) '*Great and marvellous* are thy works.'
(c) '*A high-minded man* Clarendon certainly was not, but *an able man* he undoubtedly was.'

Place the parts of these and of the following sentences in their usual order, and observe how the sentences are weakened thereby.

II. Adverbial adjunct and verb first:

(a) '*With many such parables spake* he; but *without a parable spake* he not unto them.'
(b) '*Into blood turned* he their waters.'
(c) '*Beyond all the political difficulties lay* the differences of religion.'
(d) '*So passed* the strong heroic soul away.'
(e) '*There goes* the father and *here stands* the son.'
(f) '*Now began* the revolt against the crown.'

Notice that the presence of the adverbial adjuncts renders easy the inversions in II. In prose, though not in poetry, it is both rare and difficult (except in the case of the imperative mood) to begin a sentence with a verb.

III. The object placed before the subject:

(a) '*Burghley* she did not venture to touch.'
(b) '*His passion for trifles* he dignified by the name of philosophy.'
(c) '*All these qualities* Pitt possessed in the highest degree.'
(d) '*The only real objection to the story* Croker has missed.'
(e) '*Marvellous things* did he in the sight of their fathers.'
(f) '*Him* the Almighty hurled headlong to bottomless perdition.'
(g) '*Me* he restored to my office, and *him* he hanged.'

Unless the subject or the object is a pronoun, this inversion is apt to lead to ambiguity. For example, in sentence (a), substituting 'the queen' for 'she,' we have: 'Burghley the queen did not venture to touch,' which might mean either that Burghley did not venture to touch the queen, or that the queen did not venture to touch Burghley. Consider also sentences (*c*) and (*d*).

IV. Phrase placed at the head, that is, an adjunct to a word in the body or at the end of the sentence:

(*a*) '*Of all confessors* Boswell is the most candid.'
(*b*) '*Of all generals* William was the best qualified to repair a defeat.'
(*c*) '*To his skill, energy, and presence of mind* his country owed some glorious days.'
(*d*) '*To this advice* William returned a dry answer.'
(*e*) '*On the secret motives of the emperor's conduct* it is dangerous to speculate.'
(*f*) '*On all political questions* the minister was the oracle of his own circle.'
(*g*) '*With this answer* the House was satisfied.'

The case of inversions to bring related words into proximity will be dealt with in connection with the complex sentence.

SYNTHESIS

Synthesis is the converse of analysis. In analysis we resolve the sentence into its elements; in synthesis we build up the sentence out of the elements; in analysis we dismember the sentence and thereby deprive it of symmetry and life; in synthesis we so dispose the members as to restore this symmetry and life. Synthesis is, therefore, the nobler as well as the more useful exercise.

EXAMPLE

Analysis:

Subject:	Presbyterians
Adjunct to subject:	the
Predicate:	threw
Object:	freedom
Adjunct to object:	their
Adjuncts to predicate:	1. down
	2. without casting one glance on the past
	3. at the feet of the most heartless tyrant

This is the order in which the elements of the sentence are placed in analysis, and in this form they are not only unsightly, but devoid of meaning. The analysis gives us the elements classified according to function, but nothing more.

Synthesis of the sentence :
Putting the elements together in the order of subject, predicate, object, etc., we have :

'The Presbyterians threw their freedom down without casting one glance on the past at the feet of the most heartless tyrant.'

In this form the synthesis is manifestly very faulty, for no regard is paid to the proper placement of the three qualifying adjuncts to the predicate. The writer obviously intends to lay stress on the manner in which the freedom was thrown down; the phrase *without casting one glance on the past* should therefore occupy the position of emphasis at the head of the sentence, and the single-word adjunct *down* should be placed nearer the predicate, thus :

'Without casting one glance on the past, the Presbyterians threw down their freedom at the feet of the most heartless tyrant.'

Here we have every element placed in its most effective setting ; the synthesis is therefore complete.

Observe that a comma is inserted after the adverbial adjunct placed at the head of the sentence. Punctuation is, in great measure, a matter of taste ; as a rule, however, long adverbial adjuncts placed at the head or in the body of the sentence are shut off by commas.

The adjunct placed in the body of the sentence :

(*a*) 'The public, without knowing anything whatever about the transactions of Byron's family, flew into a passion with him.'
(*b*) 'William could not, without staining his own honour, refuse to protect Sunderland.'

EXERCISE XII

Synthesise the following:

Note.—The figures in the adjuncts do not indicate the order in which the adjuncts are to be placed in the sentence; they merely number them.

No. of Sentence.	Subject.	Adjuncts to Subject.	Predicate.	Object.	Adjuncts to Object.	Adjuncts to Predicate.
1	force	1. the 2. English	was upon the Red Sea	...	...	1. again 2. before the end of May
2	Eliot	...	died	...	...	1. in the Tower 2. at the age of thirty-eight 3. three years later
3	government	the	had advanced	...	...	1. by unexpected movements 2. to the verge of war 3. step by step
4	king	the	passed	...	...	1. through Brussels 2. on his way to Spain
5	garrison	a	had been thrown	...	...	1. into Boulogne 2. during the winter

SYNTHESIS

6	Charles	…	had foreseen	impossibility	1. the 2. of an English advance	with much clearness
7	Temple	…	departed	…	…	1. after residing at Cambridge two years 2. without taking his degree
8	Temple	…	looked	…	…	1. back 2. at a later period 3. to this part of his life 4. with no great satisfaction
9	risks	1. the 2. of some mischief	were to be set	…	…	1. undoubtedly 2. against these substantial gains
10	war	1. the 2. with France	was a secondary object	…	…	to the emperor
11	everything	…	was done	…	…	1. among the polished Italians 2. by superiority of intelligence
12	division	1. the 2. of labour	had been very imperfect	…	…	1. before their time 2. in this respect
13	committee	the	resolved	to drop the prosecution	…	after a prolonged exchange of explanations
14	Walpole	…	remained	…	…	1. after leaving Court in 1717 2. in opposition 3. for three years

ENGLISH COMPOSITION

No. of Sentence.	Subject.	Adjuncts to Subject.	Predicate.	Object.	Adjuncts to Object.	Adjuncts to Predicate.
15	he	...	expressed	contempt	1. his 2. for the king's character and understanding	1. with great acrimony 2. in his official letters
16	tendency	1. the 2. to unite in such gilds	became general	...	...	1. throughout Europe 2. during the ninth and tenth centuries
17	gathering,	1. a 2. fresh 3. in arms	wrested	execution	1. the 2. full 3. of the Charter of Forests	1. from the king 2. two years later
18	tide	1. the 2. of revolution	flowed	...	...	1. on 2. upon its separate course 3. beneath the clash of hostile fleets
19	Francis	...	must be divided	...	...	1. from the emperor 2. to oppose him successfully
20	Simon	...	might have lived	...	...	1. at ease 2. on his estate 3. in modern days
21	life	Wyclif's	was saved	...	...	1. with difficulty 2. by the soldiery
22	statesman	1. the 2. great	refused	to move	...	1. at first 2. with true prudence

SYNTHESIS

23	Emperor	the	announced	intention	1. his 2. to proceed	1. immediately after the ambassador's departure 2. to the surprise of every one
24	trade	1. our 2. export 3. with that country	had increased	...	...	1. within a single year 2. with gigantic strides
25	Charles	...	declared	anxiety	1. his 2. to bring about a settlement	1. more distinctly 2. without actually threatening Francis
26	birds	these	are placed	...	...	1. now 2. on account of the structure of their feet 3. in a totally different order
27	reform	...	followed	...	...	1. now 2. with slow step and at a wide distance 3. instead of outrunning the public mind
28	question	1. the 2. of Parliamentary reform	was of very little importance	...	...	before the Revolution
29	Charles	...	must secure	support	1. the 2. of the Diet	to carry on the war successfully

No. of Sentence.	Subject.	Adjuncts to Subject.	Predicate.	Object.	Adjuncts to Object.	Adjuncts to Predicate.
30	Dr. London	...	had blundered		...	1. into perjury 2. in his eagerness to make a case against the gentlemen of the household
31	rod	the	has given	way	...	1. to the field-glass 2. by degrees (and) 3. owing to altered circumstances
32	they	...	would send	her	...	1. to London 2. without delay
33	title	a	can be gained	...	...	1. in China 2. only by success in war
34	Puritans	the	looked	...	...	1. down 2. with contempt 3. on the rich and the eloquent, on nobles and priests
35	baron	the	walked	...	...	1. with slow step and an anxious countenance 2. towards the royal pavilion

SYNTHESIS

36	troops	1. the 2. household 3. of Lewis 4. the most renowned body of fighting men in Europe	were conspicuous	in that great array
37	lad	1. a 2. of sixteen 3. Philip, son of the Duke of Orleans and nephew of the King of France	was highest	1. in rank 2. among the high-born warriors
38	provision	...	had been made	1. in the earliest ages 2. by a famous clause in the Great Charter 3. against arbitrary imprisonment
39	Parliament	...	was summoned	1. for a brief session 2. on the 19th of November of the same year 3. to authorise these steps (and) 4. to find means for the expenses of this war

No. of Sentence.	Subject.	Adjuncts to Subject.	Predicate.	Object.	Adjuncts to Object.	Adjuncts to Predicate.
40	envoy	the	gave	reason	1. a 2. more weighty 3. for refusing to proceed northwards	to his master
41	enemy	the	began	to carry out their plan	…	1. before dawn (and) 2. under cover of a thick mist
42	series	1. a 2. of columns	were thrown	…	…	1. forwards 2. against the English ridge 3. in the centre
43	column	1. the 2. Russian	was encountered	…	…	1. in the same way 2. in each case 3. by small and isolated bodies of English troops
44	general	the	brought	troops	his	1. up 2. within pistol-shot of the breastwork 3. again and again

SYNTHESIS

45	Edward	...	was the object of almost boundless admiration	...	...	1. in his own time (and) 2. among his own subjects
46	fabric	1. the 2. once beautiful	lay prostrate	...	...	1. in confused ruin 2. in a few years
47	life	1. the 2. inner 3. of the English town	was developing	itself	...	1. from the common form of life around it 2. into a form especially its own 3. in the same quiet way 4. during the progress of this outer revolution
48	story	1. a 2. chance	lights	work	1. this 2. of emancipation	1. up 2. for us 3. sometimes
49	Henry	...	had yielded	...	...	1. to the entreaties of the Privy Council 2. against his judgment
50	Johnson	...	spoke	...	...	1. of foreign travel and history 2. with the fierce and boisterous contempt of ignorance
51	we	...	have	accounts	1. but very meagre 2. of the debates in the Commons	...

No. of Sentence.	Subject.	Adjuncts to Subject.	Predicate.	Object.	Adjuncts to Object.	Adjuncts to Predicate.
52	one	1. of the most powerful of the new masters of India 2. the Viceroy of the Deccan	died	...	...	in the year 1748
53	spirit	1. Clive's 2. dauntless	shrank	...	...	1. on this occasion 2. for the first and for the last time 3. during a few hours 4. from the fearful responsibility of making a decision
54	series	1. a 2. long 3. of errors on the part of the illustrious statesman	began	...	...	now
55	citizens	1. great 2. so many	do lie	...	...	1. in no other cemetery 2. within so narrow a space

PART II

THE COMPLEX SENTENCE OF TWO CLAUSES

I. The **NOUN CLAUSE** and its Equivalents

A noun or an infinitive may be expanded into a Noun Clause.

(I.) The noun, the infinitive, and their equivalent noun clause as **Subject**:

Examples

(a) '*Mercy* becomes a monarch.'
= *To be merciful* becomes a monarch.
= *It* becomes a monarch *to be merciful.*
= *That he should be merciful* becomes a monarch.
= *It* becomes a monarch *that he should be merciful.*

It is obvious that the clause 'that he should be merciful' replaces and does the work of the noun 'mercy'; it is therefore called a *noun clause* or *a noun sentence.*

(b) '*Delay* is dangerous.'
= *To delay* is dangerous.
= *It* is dangerous *to delay.*
= *That one should delay* is dangerous.
= *It* is dangerous *that one should delay.*

The clause 'that one should delay' replaces and does the work of the noun 'delay'; hence it is called a *noun clause.*

Placed at the head of the sentence, the forms 'to be merciful,' 'that he should be merciful,' 'to delay,' 'that one should delay,' are felt to be stiff; hence, to give to a sentence of the type we are considering, a graceful poise, and to place the real subject in what is for the subject the most emphatic position in the sentence, the pronoun 'it' is placed at the beginning and the real subject at the end of the sentence. This use of 'it,' to represent vaguely something specified at the end of the sentence, should be specially noted; this is often called the *anticipatory* 'it.'

   (c) '*The education of the people* is in itself a good thing.'
     = *To educate the people* is in itself a good thing.
     = *It* is in itself a good thing *to educate the people*.
     = *That the people should be educated* is in itself a good thing.
     = *It* is in itself a good thing *that the people should be educated*.

Rule.—For the sake of variety of construction the *noun clause as subject* should be placed sometimes at the *beginning* and sometimes at the *end* of the sentence. It should be borne in mind, however, that the end is generally the position of emphasis.

The last sentence is written by its author thus: 'That the people should be educated is in itself a good thing.'

   (II.) The noun clause as **Object**:

   (a) 'Every one vowed *to defend the slayers.*'
     = Every one vowed *that he would defend the slayers.*
   (b) 'The Commons resolved *not to agree to the amendments.*'
     = The Commons resolved *that they would not agree to the amendments.*
   (c) 'He knew *how to deal with such men.*'
     = He knew *how he ought to deal with such men.*
   (d) 'I do not know *the cause of your sadness.*'
     = I do not know *why you are sad.*
     = I do not know *what has made you sad.*
   (e) 'They have forgotten *your place of residence.*'
     = They have forgotten *where you reside.*

The usual place of the objective noun clause is after the word that governs it. To make the clause emphatic it is placed before the sentence containing its governing word, as:

   (a) '*Why this was done* Temple declares himself unable to comprehend.'

'*Why this was done*,' noun clause objective, governed by 'to comprehend.' This is *parsing* the noun clause.

   (b) '*What shame meant* Wharton did not understand.'

'*What shame meant*,' noun clause objective, governed by 'did understand.'

(III.) The noun clause in **Apposition**:

(a) 'There was no danger *of his being betrayed.*'
= There was no danger *that he would be betrayed.*
(b) 'It was not easy to carry out the resolution *never to approach the queen.*'
= It was not easy to carry out the resolution *that he would never approach the queen.*

'*That he would be betrayed,*' noun clause in apposition to 'danger.'

'*That he would never approach the queen,*' noun clause in apposition to 'resolution.'

(IV.) The noun clause as **Predicate**:

(a) 'My directions were *that you should depart.*'
(b) 'Your reply is *that you were unable to go.*'

If in I., II., and III. we work backwards, we condense the clause into its equivalent noun or phrase. This interchange of equivalent constructions is obviously most useful as a device for attaining *variety* of expression in composition. It should be noted that the condensed sentence is more vigorous than the expanded sentence. 'Expanded sentence' is here used to denote the whole expression formed by the noun clause and the sentence to which this clause stands in the relation of a noun. The sentence to which the noun clause stands in the relation of a noun is called the *principal* sentence or the *principal* clause; the noun clause is sometimes called a *subordinate sentence;* and the two sentences taken together form what is called a *Complex Sentence.* A *complex sentence is one that contains a principal clause and one or more subordinate clauses.*

Subordinate clauses are of three kinds: Noun clauses, Adjective clauses, and Adverbial clauses.

Exercise I

1. Write the following sentences in as many equivalent forms as you can; expand, condense, substitute, or invert wherever you find it necessary:

It is scarcely possible to imagine anything more beautiful. Captain Fitz-Roy determined to take the boats no further. It was proposed to send off an express to summon his son to town. It would be useless waste of life to prolong the contest. That there are ten thousand thieves in London is a melancholy fact.

That such an event might happen cannot well be disputed by any one. The speech of these people scarcely deserves to be called a language. We do not see any reason for not making a few more rules of the same kind. The circumstance of its being an arm of the sea was rendered evident by the presence of several whales. They had determined to discover what had been done. The captain mentions having set a party on shore. That many of these bishops have not been bishops by apostolic succession is quite certain. He found himself at liberty to follow. He resolved to enjoy himself. He considered himself safe. He wished to retire from the business. Temple received orders to repair instantly to England. He soon found himself excluded from their secrets. The king soon told the council of his resolve to prorogue the new Parliament. That a historian should not record trifles is perfectly true. We are in no danger of being speared by the Thebans. I can't tell you the extent of my thought about this subject. The cause of his strange action was never known. The time of his coming no one can guess. We all desire happiness. The site of the city could not be discovered. They soon saw the reason for his prompt action. I cannot comprehend their refusing to work. I had not the least doubt of the man's honesty. His motive for behaving towards you in this manner is a complete puzzle to me. The queen's reasons for adopting so extraordinary a costume must be left to conjecture. Against so strong a current it was impossible to sail. There is not the slightest reason to believe the report. It deserves the praise of being a good book. How this stamping arose I cannot conjecture. War teaches men how they should die.

2. Parse the noun clauses in the following:

(*N.B.*—The clause is to be parsed as a single word. See the sentences parsed above.)

It must be owned that mere curiosity helped the success of these works. It was asked what was the writer's sex. We might say that the poet has written his own biography. He sees that our virtues have their absurd sides. It is difficult to imagine how irritating this trick becomes in the long-run. You will not suppose that I have any vulgar wish to fathom your secret. You ask if I am ready to allow myself to be convinced.

The author used to tell how the thing was done. I think that the best books in existence have all been written simply to make money. What the workmen dislike they do not know; but what they want they do know.

II. The **ADJECTIVE CLAUSE** and its Equivalents

Adjectives and adjective phrases may be expanded into equivalent clauses, and, conversely, adjective clauses may be condensed.

(I.) The **adjective** expanded into an adjective clause :

    (a) 'A *wise* man.'
    = A man *of wisdom*.
    = A man *possessing wisdom*.
    = A man *that* (or *who*) *is wise*.
    = A man *that* (or *who*) *possesses wisdom*.

'*That* (or *who*) *is wise*' and '*that* (or *who*) *possesses* wisdom' replace and do the work of the adjective 'wise'; hence they are called *adjective clauses*, or *adjective sentences*. They are also called *relative clauses*.

    (b) 'A *difficult* task.'
    = A task *of difficulty*.
    = A task *involving difficulty*.
    = A task *that* (or *which*) *is difficult*.

'*That* (or *which*) *is difficult*' replaces and does the work of the adjective 'difficult'; it is therefore an *adjective clause*.

(II.) The **possessive case** expanded into an adjective clause :

    (a) '*Byron's* poems.'
    = The poems *of Byron*.
    = The poems *written by Byron*.
    = The poems *that* (or *which*) *were written by Byron*.

'*That* (or *which*) *were written by Byron*' replaces and does the work of the possessive case 'Byron's,' and 'Byron's' does the work of an adjective; hence the clause '*that* (or *which*) *were written by Byron*' is an adjective clause. Similar remarks apply to the samples that follow.

    (b) '*His* crime.'
    = The crime *of that man*.
    = The crime *committed by that man*.
    = The crime *that* (or *which*) *was committed by that man*.
    = The crime *which that man committed*.
    = The crime *of which he was guilty*.

(III.) The **prepositional phrase** expanded into an adjective clause :

(a) 'A man *of good character.*'
= A man *having* (or *possessing*) *a good character.*
= A man *that* (or *who*) *has a good character.*
= A man *whose character is good.*
(b) 'A tree *without leaves.*'
= A tree *having no leaves.*
= A tree *that* (or *which*) *has no leaves.*
= A tree *from which the leaves have fallen.*
(c) 'Snakes possess other means *of producing sounds.*'
= Snakes possess other means *by which they can produce sounds.*

(IV.) The **participle** expanded into an adjective clause :

'Things *seen* are mightier than things *heard.*'
= Things *that* (or *which*) *are seen* are mightier than things *that* (or *which*) *are heard.*
= Things *that* (or *which*) *we see* are mightier than things *that* (or *which*) *we hear.*

The participle when placed before the noun may be regarded as a simple adjective, as :

'A *learned* man.' 'A *deserted* house.'

(V.) The **participle** with its object or its qualifying adjunct expanded into an adjective clause :

(a) 'The steam comes from the boiler *containing the water.*'
= The steam comes from the boiler *which contains the water.*
(b) 'Havelock had received from the hands of a spy a memorandum *written in Greek characters* and *describing the position and the condition of the garrison.*'
= Havelock had received from the hands of a spy a memorandum *which was written in Greek characters* and *which described the position and the condition of the garrison.*

Rule.—*The position of this species of participial phrase is* **after**, *and as* **near** *as possible to, the word to which it is an adjunct.*
This is also the place of the adjective clause.

Later on we shall meet with participial phrases performing a different function from that of those we have been considering, and for the most part occupying a different position in the sentence.

(VI.) The **adjective clause** may be condensed into a phrase or a word, as :

THE COMPLEX SENTENCE OF TWO CLAUSES

(a) 'You should carry out the orders *which your master gives you.*'
= You should carry out the orders *of your master* (or the orders *given by your master*).
= You should carry out your *master's* orders.
(b) 'This is an undertaking *that involves much labour.*'
= This is an undertaking *involving much labour.*
= This is a *laborious* undertaking.

Notice the energy of the condensed sentence.

EXERCISE II

Condense into adjectives, or adjective phrases, or expand into adjective clauses, the italicised words in the following :

A *virtuous* man. *John's* hat. *Fertile* soil. The house *on the hill* is greatly exposed. The boy brought me the stamps *that were unused.* A dog *which was half-starved* followed the boy. The man *that was the wisest* ruled the tribe. These people built little round houses *made of clay and the branches of trees.* Their houses were surrounded by a fence *of sharp stakes.* They fought with spears and axes *of flint and stone.* The leaders rode in chariots *with curved knives fastened to the wheels.* The tribes *of the south* knew how to till the soil. Many cups and ornaments have been dug out of the earth of the *burial* places. Many of *their* customs were very cruel. They used to punish those *who were guilty of theft.* He had been told of the courage *shown by the Britons.* They returned to the point *from which they had started.* Many people *in Britain* became Christians. An order was sent to *the rulers in Britain.* They hated *the cruel men who put him to death.* These men wore *coarse linen* shirts. They had on their feet thick *leather* shoes *fastened with thongs.* There are many stories told of a *famous* king *named* Arthur. Most of the tales *told about Arthur* cannot be true. Arthur was always ready to help those *who were poor or in distress.* His men had to be good and kind to *those who were weak.* They carried the king to a little chapel *standing by the sea.* The knights were left alone with the *dying* king. The ladies *on board of the barge* wept and wrung their hands. The houses *of the nobles* were at first built only of wood. Boards *resting on trestles* made the tables. The poor lived in huts *made of mud, with roofs of thatch and shingle.* The king of Mercia, *whose name was Penda,* would not believe in the religion *of Christ.* The war *with the Danes* was by no means finished. The English batteries gained the mastery over those *opposed to them*. The time *spent in landing the siege trains* had largely altered the conditions *of the contest*. The soldiers *lying under canvas* were not properly protected. This *strongly fortified* enclosure was occupied by upwards of 800 men *detached from Outram's forces*. Such facts indicate the *nation's* temper. This gentleman is a person *of sense and learning*. Iron is *of greater durability* than wood. The man's condition is *hopeless*. A stranger filled *the Stuarts' throne*. She took a husband *of her own choosing*. She was a woman *of great beauty*. Have you read *Macaulay's* essays ? The plan *laid down* appeared to have been carried out at every point. Any cruelty *caused by excess of zeal* was condoned. The view *taken of their duties* was a liberal one. The trade *with new markets not yet accustomed to receive English goods* had been chiefly *a ready-money trade*. The bank had been compelled to keep its discount *at a very high rate, varying from 6 to 9 per cent*. He gave ten pounds *for distribution among the poor*. The property *to be divided* was *of no value*. The time *of their coming* is at hand. *The motive of his action* is now to be given.

Exercise III

Parse the relative clauses in the following

(*N.B.*—The clause is to be parsed as an adjective limiting its noun or pronoun.)

All roads that lead to that end are good. I have mentioned the surprises which George Eliot sprang upon the public. One cannot suppose all readers familiar with the work which is to be the subject of discussion. Every work that comes from her pen becomes at once the event of the day. The ships of the line that our hearts love are the ships of Nelson and Collingwood and Cochrane. We are leaving behind us the security which belonged to the ages of tradition. We know the work that feudalism accomplished.

III. The **ADVERBIAL CLAUSE** and its Equivalents

It is, for the most part, difficult to replace adverbs by adverbial clauses ; but many adverbial phrases readily interchange with adverbial clauses.

(I.) **Time phrase** expanded into an adverbial clause of time:

(a) '*After experiencing a little more trouble*, we reached the peak.'
= *After we had experienced a little more trouble*, we reached the peak.
(b) 'Davison was condemned *before his trial.*'
= Davison was condemned *before he was tried.*

'After we had experienced a little more trouble' replaces and does the work of the adverbial phrase 'after experiencing a little more trouble'; and 'before he was tried' replaces and does the work of the adverbial phrase 'before his trial'; hence they are called *adverbial clauses* or *adverbial sentences*.

(II.) **Place phrase** expanded into an adverbial clause:

(a) 'I shall be glad to meet you *at my house.*'
= I shall be glad to meet you *where I live.*
(b) 'We slept *on the site of the ruined castle.*'
= We slept *where the castle once stood.*

(III.) **Manner phrase** expanded into an adverbial clause:

'Do your work *in the usual way.*'
= Do your work *as you usually do it* (or, *as you are accustomed to do it*).

(IV.) **Phrases** denoting **reason, motive, purpose, condition**, etc., expanded into adverbial clauses:

(a) 'The geese are supposed to act thus *from fear of foxes.*'
= The geese are supposed to act thus *because they fear foxes.*
(b) 'The queen blamed Buckhurst *for having executed her commands.*'
= The queen blamed Buckhurst *because he had executed her commands.*
(c) 'I have come now *for fear of not being able to come to-morrow.*'
= I have come now *lest I should not be able to come to-morrow.*
(d) 'The old man then bared his bosom *for me to return the compliment.*'
= The old man then bared his bosom *that* (or *in order that*) *I might return the compliment.*
(e) 'I dare not act *without permission from my superior officer.*'
= I dare not act *unless I get permission*, etc. (or *if I do not get permission*, etc.)
(f) 'The firing was so feeble *as to do no execution.*'
= The firing was so feeble *that it did* (or *could do*) *no execution.*
(g) 'The man was *too* lazy *to work.*'
The man was *so* lazy *that he would not work.*

If we reverse the order we condense the clause into its equivalent phrase. A very brief study of the foregoing examples will show that the condensed sentence is much more vigorous than its equivalent expanded sentence. The art of condensing is therefore more important than that of expanding. For the sake of variety of expression, however, a writer should aim at acquiring facility in both arts.

Interchange of Adverb and Adverbial Phrase

(a) 'The lawyer reasoned *well*' = The lawyer reasoned *in an able manner*.
(b) 'He spoke very *deliberately*' = He spoke *with great deliberation*.
(c) 'The house stands *there*' = The house stands *in that place*.
(d) 'I shall go *now*' = I shall go *at this moment* (or *this moment*).
(e) 'I shall *soon* know my lessons' = I shall know my lessons *in a short time*.
(f) 'You are *undoubtedly* right' = You are *without doubt* right.
(g) 'He won the prize *easily*' = He won the prize *with ease* (or *without difficulty*).
(h) 'He speaks *excitedly*' = He speaks *in an excited manner*.
(i) 'He departed *immediately*' = He departed *at once* (or *without a moment's delay*).

Exercise IV

1. Expand into phrases the adverbs in the following sentences:

You must come now. I shall go then. Our friends will soon be here. When did you arrive? Where is your brother? Why have you come? Whence comes that sound?

(*When, where, why, whence* are adverbs when used in interrogative sentences.)

Stand there. Go instantly. We bathe daily. Take her up tenderly. Do your exercise carefully. He did his work very thoroughly. They acted justly. The report is undoubtedly true. He strove manfully.

2. Expand into clauses the adverbial phrases in the following:

This apparatus was sent to me for these lectures. I open the key so as to stop the flow of the current. The gold of France was largely employed for the same purpose. Before returning they fixed a day for the meeting. The king cringed to his rivals to be able to trample on his own people. The enemy were afraid to turn for fear of being run over. After having been detained six days we put to sea on the 30th of December. Upon reaching the hill we found it the highest in the neighbourhood. With my father's permission I shall be glad to accompany you. I wished to climb the mountain to collect plants. I am deeply pained to have to tell you that I have seen your brother. On our return in the morning we were delighted to find all quiet. We could not ford the river on account of the flood. For want of money I am unable to complete the bargain.

3. Expand into clauses twenty adverbial phrases selected from your reading-book.

4. (*a*) Parse and (*b*) condense into phrases the adverbial clauses in the following:

(*N.B.*—The clause is to be parsed as a single word.)

When the morrow came the general asked for a truce that he might bury his dead. Before the time expired he was ready to capitulate. That he might avoid the use of the words 'sire' and 'majesty,' the marshal addressed himself only to the elector. While the censorship existed, no tract blaming the conduct of any public department was likely to be printed, if it had the approbation of the licenser. If there were not a general election in 1695, there must be a general election in 1696. Before he set out he paid a visit to his sister-in-law. After he had attended divine service, he took his departure. You acted as an ignorant man would act. The part of Richard the Third has become highly celebrated in England, because it has been filled by excellent performers. Where we are now standing, Temple passed the remainder of his life. If there were not a division of labour, the world could not go on. I shall visit my friends, whether you consent or not. When he walks, he moves like an engine.

5. (*a*) Parse and (*b*) condense into phrases twenty adverbial clauses selected from your reading-book.

Place of the Relative Clause

Rule.—*The place of the relative clause is* **after**, *and as* **near** *as possible to, the antecedent of the relative pronoun.*

(*Note.*—In connection with the complex sentence the young student should carefully observe *that, as a rule, the tense of the verb in the subordinate clause varies with the tense of the verb in the principal clause.*)

Examples

(*a*) 'To the arguments of this letter no one *who desired the name of Catholic prince* could reply.'

The relative clause is an adjunct to 'no one,' and is placed immediately after it, even though this placement separates, by the entire length of the adjunct, the subject of the principal clause from its predicate. By no other arrangement can the rule for the placement of relative clauses be complied with.

Variations of (*a*)

1. 'To the arguments of this letter no one could reply who desired the name of Catholic prince.'

The relative clause is here not placed as near as possible to the antecedent of the relative pronoun.

2. 'No one could reply to the arguments of this letter who desired the name of Catholic prince.'

The relative clause is more faultily placed here than in the first variation. From its present position it ought to be referred to 'letter,' and, besides this, the phrase 'to the arguments of this letter,' which is intended to be emphatic, is placed in the position of least emphasis—the middle of the sentence.

3. 'No one who desired the name of Catholic prince could reply to the arguments of this letter.'

Of the three variations this is the best; its defect lies in the placement of the adverbial adjunct 'to the arguments of this letter,' which is of sufficient importance to entitle it to be placed at the head of the sentence.

(*b*) 'The principle *on which the authors of the revolution acted* cannot be mistaken.'

The relative clause is an adjunct to 'principle,' and is placed after, and as near as possible to, the antecedent of the relative pronoun, an arrangement that can be effected only by interposing the relative clause between the subject and predicate of the principal clause. The prepositional phrase 'on which' is an adverbial adjunct to 'acted.'

Rule.—*The place of the phrase formed by a preposition and a relative pronoun is always, as here, at the head of the relative clause.*

Variations of (b)

1. 'The principle cannot be mistaken on which the authors of the revolution acted.'

The relative is too far removed from its antecedent.

2. 'The principle which the authors of the revolution acted on cannot be mistaken.'

When a preposition governs 'which' or 'whom,' the preposition and the relative should be brought together at the head of the relative clause. If, in this construction, we substitute 'that' for 'which' (or for 'whom'), the preposition is properly placed at the end of the clause, as:

'The principle that the authors of the revolution acted on cannot be mistaken.'

When 'that' is a relative it cannot be governed by a preposition placed *before* it.

3. 'The principle the authors of the revolution acted on cannot be mistaken.'

The relative 'which' or 'that' is obviously understood. This construction is not recommended.

(c) 'In the midst of these grave matters a little scene had taken place in Lambeth Chapel, *which must not be entirely forgotten.*'

The relative 'which' is too far removed from its antecedent 'scene.' The device of inversion readily enables us to bring these words together:

'In the midst of these grave matters had taken place, in Lambeth Chapel, a little scene which must not be forgotten.'

I leave another variation, an extremely faulty one, to the ingenuity of the student.

(*d*) 'By Berwick's side rode Sarsfield, *whose courage and ability earned, on that day, the esteem of the whole French army.*'

A perfect sentence. Notice (1) the inversion of the principal clause and the purpose of it, and (2) the position of the adverbial adjunct 'on that day.' This short phrase is much less important than the object with its long adjunct, and would, therefore, be entirely out of place at the end of the clause.

VARIATIONS OF (*d*)

1. 'Sarsfield rode by Berwick's side, whose courage and ability earned the esteem of the whole French army on that day.'

A most faulty sentence. The student should be able to supply the criticism. 'Whose' = 'of whom.' The sentence might therefore be written thus:

2. 'By Berwick's side rode Sarsfield, the courage and ability of whom earned, on that day, the esteem of the whole French army' (or, 'of whom the courage and ability earned,' etc.)

In this construction the interposition of the noun (or nouns) between the relative and its antecedent is not considered to mar the structure of the sentence. Yet this is not so good as (*d*).

In prose the possessive 'whose' is, by accurate writers, confined to persons. 'Of which' is the equivalent form when the antecedent denotes a thing (or things) without life, as:

(*a*) 'Men strive for those things the possession *of which* yields pleasure and consideration';

or

'Men strive for those things *of which* the possession yields pleasure and consideration';

but not

'Men strive for those things *whose* possession yields pleasure and consideration.'

(*b*) 'The two races were united under a legislation the outward form and the language *of which* were, in great measure, French.'

or '*of which* the outward form,' etc.; but not '*whose* outward form,' etc.

When in the objective case the relative is frequently omitted, as :

(a) 'They have been forced into contact with men they detest.'
= They have been forced into contact with men *whom* they detest.
(b) 'They have spent money they would rather have spared.'
= They have spent money *which* they would rather have spared.

Rule.—*The relative (or the phrase of which it forms a part) must always head the relative clause;* hence when the relative is in the objective case it precedes the subject of its own clause.

The relative clause is usually introduced by a relative pronoun; it is, however, often introduced by 'when,' 'where,' and other such relative words, as :

(a) 'My aunt showed me the seat *where* she sat.'
= My aunt showed me the seat *on which* she sat.
(b) 'We all waited anxiously for the time *when* the queen was to appear.'
= We all waited anxiously for the time *at which* the queen was to appear.
(c) 'The means *whereby* (by which) the prisoner made his escape could not be discovered.'
(d) 'The ground *whereon* (on which) thou treadest is holy ground.'
(e) 'Everybody has some point *wherein* (in which) he is especially liable to err.'
(f) 'The reason *why* (for which) he acted thus is unknown.'
(g) 'We are such stuff *as* (which) dreams are made of' (='of which dreams are made').

The relative 'as,' like the relative 'that,' cannot be governed by a preposition placed before it.

(h) 'Such things *as* (which) I require I shall bring with me.'

Here 'as' is the object of the verb in the relative clause 'as I require.' After 'such' and 'same,' 'as' has the force of a relative.

But' after a negative adverb has the force of a relative. 'But' used in this way = 'which—not,' 'who—not.'

(i) '(There is) not a blade of grass *but* has its story to tell, not a heart *but* has its romance, not a life which does not hide a secret.'
= (There is) not a blade of grass *which* has *not* its story to tell, not a heart *which* has *not* its romance, not a life which does not hide a secret.

Notice that, in the last clause of this sentence, the usual construction is adopted. Instead of *not a life which does not hide a secret*, the author might have written *not a life but hides a secret.* The change of construction, however, helps to make this clause, what the author intended it to be, the most emphatic in the sentence.

Make sentences of your own in which 'but' = 'who—not' or 'which—not.'

(*j*) 'Things are not what they seem.'

Here 'what they seem' is a noun clause used as the predicate of the sentence; or we may consider 'what' as equal to 'that which,' in which case 'that' is a demonstrative pronoun and the predicate of the principal clause. 'Things are not that' and 'which they seem' is an adjective clause to 'that.' In most cases, however, there is no necessity for resolving 'what' into 'that which' or 'those which.'

(*k*) 'In the first moment she felt ashamed of *what her husband had done.*'

'What her husband had done' is here a noun clause governed by the preposition 'of.'

(*l*) '*What they saw* was lovely enough to have kept any one at gaze.'

Here 'what they saw' is a noun clause and the subject of the sentence. Resolve 'what' into 'that which' and observe how the sentence is enfeebled.

NOTE ON THE RELATIVE CLAUSE

Professor Bain recommends that the relative clause that is intended to limit or define the antecedent should invariably be introduced by 'that,' and that the relative clause that is intended only to add another fact or circumstance should be introduced by 'who' or 'which.'

I. Examples in which the relative clause limits or defines the antecedent:

(*a*) 'This is the house that Jack built.'

Whose house? What house? The function of the clause 'that Jack built' is to tell what house is referred to. It excludes every house except the one built by Jack. The application of the antecedent is therefore *restricted* or *limited* by the relative clause.

(b) 'Cats that wear gloves catch no mice.'

As a matter of fact cats do catch mice. What cats, then, are referred to in this sentence ? The clause 'that wear gloves' answers the question. It *restricts* the cats that do not catch mice to those that wear gloves.

The relative clause that defines and limits the antecedent is called the **Restrictive Relative Clause.**

II. Examples in which the relative introduces a clause that adds another fact *without defining or limiting the antecedent*:

(a) 'I gave the pen to my sister, who lost it.'

Here the relative clause adds another fact, namely, that my sister lost the pen, but does not define or limit the antecedent 'sister,' which is sufficiently definite without the clause. The sense is:

'I gave the pen to my sister, and she lost it' ('who'='and she').

(b) 'These animals are killed for their fat, which is made into oil.'

Here again the relative clause adds another fact, namely, that the fat of these animals is made into oil, but does not define or limit the antecedent 'fat.' The sense is:

'These animals are killed for their fat, and it (the fat) is made into oil' ('which'='and it').

'Which' and 'who,' when used in this way, are called *co-ordinating or continuative relatives*, and the clauses they introduce are called *co-ordinating or continuative clauses*.

It is to this use that Bain would restrict 'who' and 'which.' He argues his case with great skill and wealth of illustration, but is forced to admit that 'many good writers use "who" and "which," as well as "that," for the restrictive meaning.' It would certainly conduce to clearness to adopt his recommendation ; and, whether we adopt it or not, we should carefully keep in mind the dual function of the relative clause.

Which, like **it**, may have a large part, or the whole, of a clause for its antecedent, as :

(a) 'Mr. Grenville lost America because he read the American despatches, which none of his predecessors ever did' ('which' = the reading of the despatches).

(b) 'Cæsar crossed the Rubicon, which was in effect a declaration of war' ('which' = the fact that Cæsar crossed the Rubicon = the crossing of the Rubicon by Cæsar).

Syntax of the Relative Pronouns

Which applies to things and lower animals; **that** to things, lower animals, and persons; and **who** only to persons. Like the other pronouns, *they agree with their antecedents in number, person, and gender.*

Examples

(a)

1st person singular:

'*I who speak am* your commander.'

2nd person singular:

'*Thou who speakest art* my commander.'

3rd person singular:

'*He who speaks is* your commander.'

1st person plural:

'*We who speak are* your commanders.'

2nd person plural:

'*You who speak are* my commanders.'

3rd person plural:

'*Those (they) who speak are* my commanders.'

(b) 'They will not allow the author to rank with *those great men who* have bequeathed to posterity *models which* defy imitation.'

'Who' represents 'those great men,' 'which' represents 'models'; each of them represents a plural noun of the 3rd person, each of them is in the nominative case, and each of them takes a verb of the *same person and number* as its antecedent.

(c) '*Thou who hast* so short a time to live, art thou already weary?'

'Thou,' the antecedent of 'who,' is 2nd person singular,

therefore 'who' is 2nd person singular, and the verb 'hast' is 2nd person singular, to agree with its antecedent 'who.'

As a rule, when the relative is the subject of its clause, the number of its antecedent is the most important point in agreement to note; *for the number of the verb of the relative clause is, in this case, determined by the number of the antecedent of the relative pronoun.*

The writer of the following sentence has not referred the relative to its antecedent, and has consequently used in the relative clause a verb that does not agree in number with the antecedent of the relative pronoun:

> 'Mr. Dodsley this year brought out his *Preceptor*, one of the most valuable books for the improvement of young minds *that has* appeared in any language.'

The writer has referred 'that' to 'one' instead of to 'books.'

> 'Many most valuable books for the improvement of the young *have* appeared, and Dodsley's *Preceptor* is one of them.'

THE AND WHICH AND AND WHO BLUNDER

EXAMPLES

> (a) 'I have a book, printed at Antwerp, *and which* was once possessed by Adam Smith.'

'Which' joins the relative clause, and does not need 'and' to assist it.

> 'I have a book, printed at Antwerp, which was once possessed by Adam Smith.'

Or expand into a clause the participial phrase 'printed at Antwerp':

> 'I have a book *which* was printed at Antwerp, *and which* was once possessed by Adam Smith.'

Here 'and' is correctly used, for its function is *to join together two relative clauses that refer to the same antecedent.*

> (b) 'All the rights of the people were absorbed into the hands of the conqueror, *and who* added the title of king to that of conqueror.'

'Who' is able, without the assistance of 'and,' to join its own clause to the principal clause; 'and' should therefore be deleted.

(c) 'The second assertion imputes the evil to a cause in itself inevitable, *and which* has only partially operated in producing it.'

Here there is but one relative clause; hence, as the sentence stands, 'and' is not needed. Notice, however, that the phrase 'in itself inevitable' is really a *condensed* relative clause. Expand the phrase thus: 'which is in itself inevitable.' Substituting the clause for the phrase, we have:

'The second assertion imputes the evil to a cause *which* is in itself inevitable, *and which* has only partially operated in producing it.'

Now we have two relative clauses referring to the same antecedent, and the second clause is joined to the first by 'and'; the conjunction 'and' is therefore correctly used.

Do not write: **they who** or **them who**, but **those who**, as:

(a) '*Those who* thought only of liberty deserved to be Romans.'
(b) 'It is right that man should love *those who* have offended him.'

In relative clauses do not substitute another part of speech for the relative pronoun.

EXAMPLES

(a) 'I have read of a man who was very rich, but *he* was very miserly.'

'But' is here intended to join a second relative clause. The sentence should read:

'I have read of a man who was very rich, but *who* was very miserly.'

(b) 'Hill is one of the few surviving magistrates of the island, of which he is a native, and has lived *in it* all his life.'

'And' is intended to join two relative clauses, viz. 'of which he is a native' and '*in which he* has lived all his life.'

(c) 'Will you sweeten the lives of suffering men by the thought of a being whose mercy is not as our mercy, nor *his* justice as our justice, nor *his* fatherhood as the fatherhood of men?'

THE COMPLEX SENTENCE OF TWO CLAUSES

The clauses joined by 'nor' are intended to be relative clauses to 'being'; hence 'his' should in each case be 'whose.'

As a rule, the relative should be repeated when it is the subject of more than one clause, as:

> 'We have ourselves heard old men, *who* knew nothing of Clive's history, but *who* still retained the prejudices conceived in their youth, talk of him as an incarnate fiend.'

A noun or a pronoun in the possessive case is functionally an adjective, and therefore should not be made the antecedent of a relative pronoun. This rule is departed from in the following examples:

> (a) 'The sight of *his* blood whom they deemed invulnerable, shook the courage of the soldiers.'

Write:
> 'The sight of the blood of *him* whom,' etc.

> (b) 'We glorify *his* name and mission who was the Prince of Peace.'

Write:
> 'We glorify the name and mission of *him* who,' etc.

The young student should be careful not to write 'whom' without assuring himself that it is governed either by a preposition or by a verb. 'Whom' is improperly employed in the following examples:

> (a) 'These are the persons *whom* I thought were far away.'

This is a sentence of three clauses:

> (1) These are the persons.
> (2) I thought.
> (3) *Whom* were far away.

The analysis shows that 'whom' ought to be *who*.

> (b) 'I am speaking of young Harper, *whom* we all agree was rather nice-looking.'

Here we have another sentence of three members:

> (1) I am speaking of young Harper.
> (2) We all agree.
> (3) *Whom* was rather nice-looking.

It is obvious that 'whom' should be *who*.

In the following sentence 'who' is improperly used for 'whom.'

'This is my father, who Penelope told me she had seen brushing the dust off an old rocking-horse.'

The clauses of the sentence are:

(1) This is my father.
(2) Penelope told me.
(3) She had seen who brushing, etc.

'Had seen' is transitive and 'who' is its object; 'who' should therefore be 'whom.'

Exercise V

Correct the errors in the following sentences, and give reasons for your corrections:

1. He attempted to commit suicide by firing a pistol at his head, which he had concealed amongst the bedclothes.
2. There are objections to the purchase and working of railways and canals by the State with which we are sufficiently familiar in England (ant. of 'which' is 'objections').
3. They who have talents want industry or virtue; they who have industry want talents.
4. Why should they practise arts of cunning who have nothing to fear?
5. Such are a few of the many paradoxes one could cite from his writings, and which are now before me.
6. There are certain general conditions and principles common to all histories, and which are essential to enable us to explain the facts.
7. Shakespeare frequently has lines and passages in a strain quite false, and which are entirely unworthy of him.
8. Nothing can hinder this *History* from being one of the most considerable books which has appeared for the last ten years.
9. Valencia is one of the most delightful cities which is to be found in Europe.
10. It is a doctrine not very easily adapted to his habitual creed, and which drops out of his mind whenever he passes from external nature and himself.

11. The position of Thomson was very different, in whom we meet with a most original poetic figure.

12. To early English poetry he was mainly giving his attention, of which he intended to write a history.

13. The heroine of this book is a young girl, who describes in letters to her father and mother what goes on in the house of a lady who she had lived with as maid and who is just dead.

14. There is that little prig Blifil, who only a generous mind could have created.

15. Of these pretenders it is fit to distinguish those who endeavours to deceive from them who is deceived.

16. In the afternoon the old gentleman proposed a walk to Vauxhall, a place of which he had heard much, but had never seen it.

17. He is the sort of man who compels respect, and who one might even love.

18. He learned much from his master's example, who was very kind to him.

19. Precision imports pruning the expression so as to exhibit neither more nor less than an exact copy of his idea who uses it.

20. The more accurately we search into the human mind, the stronger traces we find of his wisdom who made it.

21. Nina was annoyed by the presence of Mr. Jekyl, whom her brother insisted should remain to dinner.

22. This is the man whom I heard had gone to Australia.

23. We had the pleasure of Mr. and Mrs. Oswell's company, whom we thought were delightful people.

24. I should esteem the man a coward, whom I might pity, but I don't think I could love him.

25. This prevents their attending enough to what is in the Bible, and makes battle for what is not in the Bible, but they have put it there.

26. It peoples caves with deities, to whom it not only gives a local habitation, but paints their forms and tunes their voices.

27. We are his bondsmen who bought us.

28. Everywhere we find strong traces of his wisdom who made us.

29. I confess that I am not one of those who am unable to refuse my assent to these conclusions.

Place of the Adverbial Clause

I. Place of the **Time-Clause**.

Clauses introduced by 'when,' 'while,' 'whenever,' 'before,' 'after,' are *usually* placed *before* the clause they qualify.

Examples

(a) '*When Byron attacked any one*, he brought his whole soul to the work.'
(b) '*While the king was disquieted by the conduct of the Northern Powers*, ominous signs began to appear in another quarter.'
(c) '*Whenever you meet with a difficulty*, do your best to overcome it.'
(d) '*Before Temple left England*, he had a long audience of the king.'
(e) '*After the vote was taken*, the members dispersed.'

II. Place of the **Conditional** and the **Concessive Clause**.

Clauses introduced by 'if,' 'though,' 'although,' and other words implying condition or concession, are *usually* placed *before* the clause they qualify.

Examples

(a) '*If Charles had succeeded in his scheme of governing without a parliament*, the consequence of the Peers would have been grievously diminished.'
(b) '*Had such changes appeared in their natural place*, we should leave them to their natural fate' (= If such changes had appeared, etc.)
(c) '*Though the direction of their passions was altered*, the violence of those passions was the same.'
(d) '*Provided you do your duty*, no one will complain.'
(e) '*Few as they were*, the English fought desperately' (= Though they were few, etc.)
(f) '*Whatever the consequence may be*, I shall resolutely do my duty.'
(g) '*However fair may be his promises*, the man is not to be trusted.'

III. The place of the **Clause of Reason**.

(1) Clauses introduced by 'because' and 'for' are *usually* placed *after* the clause they qualify.

Examples

(a) 'I have come back *because I could not stay away.*'
(b) 'His set speeches were always his worst, *for in these his want of taste at once came to the front.*'

(2) Clauses introduced by 'as' (= since), 'since,' 'seeing that,' 'considering that,' are *usually* placed *before* the clause they qualify.

Examples

(a) '*As* (= *since*) *Bute was known to be his master's mouthpiece*, a peace-party was at once formed.'
(b) '*Since we have referred to his literary tastes*, it would be unjust not to praise his encouragement of liberal studies.'
(c) '*Seeing that you have been fairly beaten*, you should cheerfully acknowledge your defeat.'
(d) '*Considering that your task was one of great difficulty*, you have done exceedingly well.'

The adverbial clause, like the adverb and the adverbial phrase, readily lends itself to transposition from one part of the sentence to another, and, like them, is peculiarly apt to be misplaced. In a sentence of only two short clauses its placement is often of no great importance; but, as we shall see later on, in a long sentence of three or more clauses we should be careful so to place it as to make it bear most effectively on the part of the sentence we intend it to qualify.

IV. Adverbial clauses of **Consequence** and of **Comparison**.

These clauses *usually follow* the clause they qualify.

Examples of the Clause of Consequence

(a) 'The king was so feeble *that he might safely be suffered to encroach.*'

Or:

'So feeble was the king *that he might,*' etc.

The inversion of the principal clause makes the predicate 'feeble' emphatic.

(b) 'So intense was the greed of gain *that only a threat of death could keep the fighting men in their ranks.*'

The Clause of Comparison, comprising Clauses of Defect, Excess, and Equality

(1) The clause expressing **defect**.

EXAMPLES

(a) 'Other countries have been more enterprising *than we have been (enterprising)*.'
(b) 'It is better to have an imperfect knowledge *than none at all*' (=than it is good to have none at all).

(2) The clause expressing **excess**.

EXAMPLES

(a) 'John is less able *than James*' (=than James is able).
(b) 'Carlyle had less faith in the "Balance of Power" *than had Byron*' (=than Byron had little faith in the 'Balance of Power').

The meaning is: Byron had little faith in the 'Balance of Power,' and Carlyle had less faith in it.

By inverting the order of the members of these sentences we may make the member introduced by 'than' one of defect, as:

(a) 'James is more able *than John*.'
(b) 'Byron had more faith in the "Balance of Power" *than had Carlyle*.'

The member or clause introduced by 'than' is generally much contracted, a fact that is apt to lead to ambiguity. It was to avoid ambiguity that the author of the last sentence interposed 'had' between 'than' and 'Carlyle.'

In this light consider the following:

> 'Henry admired James more than John.'

This might mean either that 'Henry admired James more than he admired John,' or that 'Henry admired James more than John admired James.' If the former is intended to be the meaning we should write, 'Henry admired James more than he did John'; and if the latter is intended to be the meaning we should write, 'Henry admired James more than did John' (or, more than John did).

Other Examples

(a) 'He likes you better *than me*' (=than he likes me).
(b) 'He likes you better *than I*' (=than I like you).
(c) 'He that loves father or mother more *than me* is not worthy of me' (=than he loves me).
(d) '*Phrases rule the world more *than ideas*.'

Better say: 'More than do ideas,' or 'more than ideas do.'

(e) 'His trial was not greater *than hundreds of others had borne with constancy*.'

A very faulty sentence. There can be no comparison (in the sense in which 'comparison' is here employed) between a man's 'trial' and 'hundreds of other (people).' We can compare 'trials' with 'trials,' and 'people' with 'people,' but not 'trials' with 'people.' The sentence should read :

'His trial was not greater than were those which hundreds of others had borne with constancy.'

Than is sometimes improperly used for **when**, as :

(a) 'I had scarcely passed a projecting crag, *than* there occurred an explosion.'
(b) 'Hardly had misconduct in one shape succumbed to treatment, *than* it broke out in another.'

In these sentences 'when' should be substituted for 'than.' The function of 'than' is to introduce a standard of comparison, not a clause of time.

(3) The clause expressing **equality**.

Examples

(a) 'He could rail as well *as he could praise*.'
(b) 'France is longing for victory quite as much *as for her Provinces*' (=as she is longing for her Provinces).
(c) 'To desire this consummation was as natural *as to desire a treaty with Spain*' (=as to desire a treaty with Spain was natural).
(d) 'He speaks *as he thinks*.'

Or better thus :

'*As he thinks*, so he speaks.'

This inversion is sometimes very effective:

'*As the hart panteth after water-brooks*, so panteth my soul after thee.'

The combination of the comparison of equality with that of defect frequently leads to error.

EXAMPLES

(a) 'He is *as tall* or *taller than* his brother.'
= He is as tall than his brother, or he is taller than his brother.

When the comparisons are combined as in (a), the following is the form:

'He is as tall as or taller than his brother.'

(b) 'The subterranean rumblings were more frequent and of longer duration, but not so loud *as during the previous day*.'

The comparatives 'more frequent' and 'longer' should be followed by 'than,' not by 'as.' Thus:

'The subterranean rumblings were more frequent and of longer duration than, but not so loud as, during the previous day.'
(= than (they were frequent and of long duration during the previous day) but not so loud as (they were loud) during the previous day).

In comparative constructions what we have to remember is:

1. That the comparative degree of the adjective and the adverb is followed by a clause introduced by **than**.

2. That 'not so' and 'as' are followed by a clause introduced by **as**.

(4) The clause expressing **proportionate equality** is *usually* placed *before* the clause it qualifies.

EXAMPLES

(a) '*The more you practise*, the better will you play.'
(= By so much more you practise, by so much better you will play.)

'The' is, in this construction, an adverb of degree.

(b) '*The nearer the bone*, the sweeter the meat.'

V. The place of the Clause of Purpose.

The clause of purpose sometimes *precedes* and sometimes *follows* the clause it qualifies.

EXAMPLES

(a) 'Honour thy father and thy mother, *that thy days may be long.*'
(b) 'Spare me a little, *that I may recover my strength.*'
(c) '*That they might check the influence of wealth,* they yearly produced a motion in favour of ballot at elections.'

NOTE ON DO AND SO

In the subordinate clause of the comparative construction the verb 'to do' is often substituted for the verb used in the principal clause.

EXAMPLES

(a) 'He spoke as well as you *did*' (= as you spoke well).
(b) 'He spoke as well as you could have *done*' (= as you could have spoken well).
(c) 'We work harder than he *does*' (= than he works hard).

'So' may represent a word, a phrase, or a clause. Its useful representative character is shown in the following examples:

(a) 'I am fortunate, and *so* is my brother.'
   = I am fortunate, and my brother is also fortunate.
(b) 'We were in danger, and *so* were you.'
   (So = in danger.)
(c) 'Thou art thy father's daughter; there's enough. *So* was I, when you took his dukedom.'
   (So = my father's daughter.)
(d) 'The handwriting of the age is unsatisfactory; *so* say the press and the people.'
   (So = the handwriting of the age is unsatisfactory.)

DO AND SO IN COMBINATION

(a) 'Can we show that muscle is the seat of chemical changes? If we can *do so*, we may find that there are operations going on in muscle that are comparable to combustion in the furnace of a steam-engine.'
   (Do so = show that muscle is the seat of chemical changes.)
(b) 'I would cut off my left hand with my right, could my *doing so* attest my sincerity.'
   (Doing so = cutting off my left hand with my right.)

NOTE ON **THE COMPARISONS**

Consider the following examples:

(a) 'I like it better than any.'
= I like it better than I like any.

'Any' ought to include 'it'; hence the comparison is between *things included in the same class*. This comparison is the work, not of the comparative, but of the superlative degree. If 'it' is intended to be included in 'any' we should write, 'I like it the best of all'; but if 'it' and 'any' are intended to refer to different classes of things, we should write, 'I like it better than any *other*.' Here 'other' excludes 'it' from the group or class of things denoted by 'any.'

The comparative *excludes* from the same class, and the superlative *includes* in the same class, the things compared. Neglect of this distinction frequently leads to error.

(b) 'Mazzini may be said to have done more for the unity of Italy than any living man.'

When this sentence was written Mazzini was alive; hence 'Mazzini' and 'living man' were at that time included in the same class, viz. the class *living men*. As the sentence stands, however, the comparative 'more' excludes Mazzini from that class; but the writer intended to exclude him, not from the class *living men*, but from the class *other living men*. He should have written:

'Mazzini may be said to have done more for the unity of Italy than any *other* living man.'

Or:

'Of living men (or, of all living men) Mazzini may be said to have done the most for the unity of Italy.'

(c) 'Eve was the fairest of her daughters.'

The superlative should be used only when *the second term of the comparison includes the first*. Eve, the mother, cannot be included in the class *her daughters*; hence the sentence involves an absurdity. Write:

'Eve was fairer than her daughters.'
'Eve was fairer than any of her daughters.'
'Eve was fairer than the fairest of her daughters.'

Or :

> 'Eve was the fairest of women.'

The second term 'women' obviously includes the first term 'Eve.'

(d) 'He was the most able of all his predecessors.'

The second term of the comparison does not include the first, for a man cannot be one of his predecessors; but the sentence makes him one, therefore it is absurd. Write :

> 'He was more able than any of his predecessors.'

Or :

> 'Of all his predecessors none was so able as he.'

Exercise VI

Correct the following, and give reasons for the changes you make :

John is cleverer than any boy in his class. May writes better than any girl of her age. We are apt to think our manners the best of all others. Lamb's letters make up a volume of more interest than any book. He is better versed in history than any living man. An Englishman is just as serious in sports as in any act of his life. Nothing that remains in any part of the world is so perfect as these temples. On this subject no person ought to think with so much charity of others, or to speak with greater diffidence than myself. No one ever wounded himself more madly, or so causelessly as he. It is said that nothing was so teasing to Lord Erskine than being addressed by his second title. She gathered as many flowers, and even more than she wanted. Such women generally marry men as young or younger than themselves. This explorer was the only one of his predecessors who slaughtered the natives of the region he passed through.

ANALYSIS OF COMPLEX SENTENCES

Analyse:

(1) He says things as no one else says them, in a manner at once strange and striking.
(2) This lady has published half a dozen books, each one of which is a masterpiece.

Kind of Clause.	Connective.	Subject.	Adjuncts to Subject.	Predicate.	Object.	Adjuncts to Object.	Adjuncts to Predicate.
A Principal		he		says	things	...	1. clause (a) 2. in a manner at once strange and striking
(a) Adv. to 'says' in A	as	no one	else	says	them	...	...
A Principal	...	lady	this	has published	books	half a dozen clause (a)	...
(a) Rel. to 'books' in A	which	one	1. each 2. of which	is a masterpiece	...	...	...

Exercise VII

1. Analyse the following:

(*N.B.*—Carefully note the position of the subordinate clause; and, where possible, invert the order of the clauses and observe the effect of the inversion.)

Such is the ground on which our author takes his stand. Which of us has any notion of the intellectual activity that occupies his neighbours? As soon as Sterne had graduated, he was provided with a benefice. When the poor woman left York to join him, he could not find time to look at her. If we keep the sense of the work, we must give up its form. In such straits does the critic find himself when he tries to interpret between two languages. This writer has attempted nothing in which he has not excelled. The intelligence demands novelty as the body demands action. I think your pathos better than your fun. We are as happy as princes. Would not her genius desert her when she left the scenes of rustic life in England? We are most anxious that you should stay here for the night. No sooner did Maximus appear in the street than he was destroyed by the populace. The more we read of the history of past ages, the more we observe the signs of our own times. If I were a nightingale, I would discharge the office of a nightingale. Slow as the progress seemed, the colonies were really growing fast in numbers and in wealth. His nature was as brave as it was tender. Keen as was his love of power, no man ever refused office so often. We are the more inclined to credit this story, because Mr. Gleig does not contradict it. Although it was a week-day night, yet the fame of the preacher drew a very fair congregation. Whatever he was, he was not a hypocrite. Were I to die to-morrow, my daughter would in all probability have absolutely nothing. If you have quite decided, I congratulate you, my dear. Have you seen the archdeacon since you left us? By three o'clock we were assembled in the minster, the nave of which was crowded from end to end. Whether he slept at all that night I cannot say. How he passed the next two or three days, the rector could hardly have told. Whether he acted wisely or not, it would be difficult to decide. The excitement in a place where excitements were so rare became almost intense. The emperor was at the head of a body, the members of which were seldom in harmony. Not a few of the authors in vogue had the honour of having attributed to them a book which certainly none of them was capable of writing. The reader is carried along by the rapidity with which one event follows another. Nor was Shakespeare one of those whose merit is unrecognised till long after their own day. Not a play of his but shows some intention of high teaching. Sterne tries to be odd, which is the worst way of attaining oddity. So frightened was Burleigh at the exhibition of feeling, that he despaired of Elizabeth's surviving the storm. The coming of the Armada was the last act of which the divorce of Queen Catherine was the first. Hardly any seat against which a petition is brought can be considered perfectly safe. The welfare of the country required an act of severity with which the queen would herself have gladly dispensed. The terms of the resolution implied that the queen should be troubled no further. The thicker they were crowded, the less easy would they find it to move. Teachers of divinity differ more among themselves than teachers of any other subject. There is nothing more inspiring to the mind of man than religious enthusiasm. Although he slay me, yet will I trust him. This is the kind of thing we meet with in this wondrous forest. We are bound to give our children the best we have. Wages, Mr. Harrison declares, have gone up 1 per cent. How far each country has solved its educational problem is a matter for interesting discussion. Whether the professor's results will be generally accepted is perhaps a matter of doubt. Every one will recognise the skill and ability with which he handles his subject. Where had I seen eyes of which these reminded me? Only one thing would I urge, that he be allowed a free hand. This is the favour that I came to ask. Down from the beetling crag to which he clung, tumbled the tawny rascal.

2. Re-write the foregoing sentences, changing the present tense of the verb for the past, or the past for the present, as:

Present

Such *is* the ground on which our author *takes* his stand.

Past

Such *was* the ground on which our author *took* his stand.

Past (perfect)

This writer *had attempted* nothing in which she *had not excelled*.

Present (perfect)

This writer *has attempted* nothing in which she *has not excelled*.

SYNTHESIS OF COMPLEX SENTENCES OF TWO CLAUSES

Analysed Complex Sentences of Two Clauses

Kind of Clause.	Connective.	Subject.	Adjuncts to Subject.	Predicate.	Object.	Adjuncts to Object.	Adjuncts to Predicate.
A Principal	...	circumstances	1. the 2. two 3. clause (a)	took	turn	1. a 2. new	1. suddenly 2. to the great dismay of the Jacobites
(a) Rel. to 'circumstances' in A	which	they		had been counting	...	...	1. so fondly 2. on which
A Principal	...	he		felt	clause (a)	...	
(a) Noun to 'felt' in A	that	he		might give	offence	much	1. by refusing help to the king 2. to a powerful neighbour
A Principal	...	something	...	might be expected	...	...	1. from his exhaustion 2. clause (a)
(a) Adv. to 'might be expected' in A	though	confidence	little	could be placed			in the king's good faith

Synthesis of these three Analysed Sentences

No. I.

Principal clause : The two circumstances suddenly took a new turn, to the great dismay of the Jacobites
Relative clause : they had been so fondly counting on which.

The clauses combined :
The relative must be as near as possible to its antecedent 'circumstances'; hence we may write :

'The two circumstances on which they had been so fondly counting suddenly took a new turn, to the great dismay of the Jacobites.'

Notice (1) that in its present position the long adverbial phrase 'to the great dismay of the Jacobites' makes the sentence 'draggle,' and (2) that this phrase is intended to bring into prominence the effect produced by the altered circumstances. It should therefore be placed at the head thus :

'To the great dismay of the Jacobites, the two circumstances on which they had been so fondly counting suddenly took a new turn.'

No. II.

Principal clause : He felt
Noun clause : that he might give much offence to his powerful neighbour by refusing help to the king.

The noun clause is, as it now stands, badly balanced ; it has one word before and twelve words after the predicate, and it has at the end the adverbial phrase 'by refusing help to the king,' which is intended sweepingly to qualify the whole clause. Placing this phrase in the position in which it can discharge its function most effectively, we have :

'He felt that, by refusing help to the king, he might give much offence to his powerful neighbour.'

No. III.

Principal clause : Something might be expected from his exhaustion
Adverbial clause : though little confidence could be placed in the king's good faith.

The concessive clause is usually placed before the clause it modifies ; hence we should combine the clauses thus :

'Though little confidence could be placed in the king's good faith, something might be expected from his exhaustion.'

Or, transposing 'king's' and 'his,' we may write:

'Something might be expected from the king's exhaustion, though little confidence could be placed in his good faith.'

In the first combination the sense is *suspended* until the close of the sentence. The mind is not satisfied until the last word is reached. Sentences in which the sense is thus suspended are called *periodic* sentences, and the construction by which the suspense is produced is called the *periodic construction*. The periodic sentence is obviously produced by placing the qualifying clause before the clause that it qualifies.

In the second combination there is no suspension of the sense. The mind is satisfied at 'exhaustion.' A sentence of this type is called a *loose* sentence.

EXERCISE VIII

Synthesise the following analysed sentences:

(*Note.*—The adverbial clause, if of considerable length, should be shut off from the principal clause, by a comma.)

ANALYSED COMPLEX SENTENCES OF TWO CLAUSES

(The number in ( ) indicates the consecutive number of the sentence.)

Kind of Clause.	Connective.	Subject.	Adjuncts to Subject.	Predicate.	Object.	Adjuncts to Object.	Adjuncts to Predicate.
(1) A Principal	...	English	the	took	refuge	...	1. in incredulity 2. clause (a)
(a) Adv. to 'took' in A	while	Charles		was enjoying	success	his	
(2) A Principal	...	guns	1. the 2. heavy 3. clause (a)	had been mounted	...	...	on the ramparts
(a) Rel. to 'guns' in A	which	they	...	had used	which	...	in the siege

ANALYSED COMPLEX SENTENCES

(3) A Principal		English	the	had been idle	...	...	1. not 2. in the three weeks of possession 3. clause (a)
(a) Adv. to the predicate of A	though	fortifications	the	were unrepaired	...	...	still
(4) A Principal		adventure	the	might have been pardoned	...	...	clause (a)
(a) Adv. to predicate of A	if	it		had formed	close	1. the 2. of a series of successes	
(5) A Principal		Sir James		possessed	qualities	1. the 2. intellectual and moral 3. clause (a)	in a very high degree
(a) Rel. to 'qualities' in A	which	which		are most important			in a historian

ENGLISH COMPOSITION

Kind of Clause.	Connective.	Subject.	Adjuncts to Subject.	Predicate.	Object.	Adjuncts to Object.	Adjuncts to Predicate.
(6) A Principal	...	tenderness	1. that 2. to the fallen 3. clause (a)	was discernible	...	...	1. hardly 2. for a time
(a) Rel. to 'tenderness' in A	which	which	...	has been a marked feature of the national character	...	...	through many generations
(7) A Principal	...	ancestors	our	knew	clause (a)	...	from the experience of several generations at home and abroad
(a) Noun to predicate of A	how	disposition	1. the 2. of the Church	was restless and encroaching	...	...	how
(8) A Principal	...	we	...	place	Toleration Act	the	foremost in the list of benefits, clause (a)
(a) Rel. to 'benefits'; in A	which	country	our	owes	which	...	to the Revolution

ANALYSED COMPLEX SENTENCES

(9) A Principal	...	history	1. the 2. of the faction, clause (a)	is interesting or pleasing	...		by no means
Rel. to 'faction' in A	which	which		divided	court and council	her her	towards the close of the reign of Elizabeth
(10) A Principal		Italians	the	were acquainted	...		with all the follies of his youth and with all the dishonest arts, clause (a)
Rel. to 'arts' in A	which	he		had attained	power		by which
(11) A Principal	...	practice	1. the 2. of employing mercenaries	became universal	...	... — ...	1. in the north of Italy 2. at a time, clause (a)
Rel. to 'time' in A	when	it		was unknown			1. almost 2. in other countries 3. when = in which

Kind of Clause.	Connective.	Subject.	Adjuncts to Subject.	Predicate.	Object.	Adjuncts to Object.	Adjuncts to Predicate.
(12) A Principal	...	stretch	1. a 2. of pasture-land, clause (a)	lies	...	...	beyond the woodland
(a) Rel. to 'land' in A	which	which	...	brings	you	...	to the foot of the long ridge of hills forming the eastern boundary of the plain
(13) A Principal	...	road	1. the 2. post 3. clause (a)	ran	...	...	up this ravine
(a) Rel. to 'road' in A	which	which	...	passed	...	...	1. along the neck and 2. through the centre of the English lines
(14) A Principal	...	series	1. that 2. long 3. of Oriental triumphs 4. clause (a)	commences	...	...	with the defence of Arcot
(a) Rel. to 'series' in A	which	which	closes	...	...	...	with the fall of Ghizni

ANALYSED COMPLEX SENTENCES

(15) A Principal	...	birds	1. a 2. few 3. clause (a)	may be seen	...	1. now and then 2. on these hills
(a) Rel. to 'birds' in A	which	we	...	meet	...	1. with which 2. in the lower grounds 3. seldom
(16) A Principal (interrogative)	...	it	clause (a) (real subj.)	is a source of mortification	...	1. not 2. to men
(a) Noun real subj. of A	that	they	...	are excluded	...	from political power
(17) A Principal	...	sovereign	the	threw	chiefs	1. the 2. of the opposition 3. into prison 4. clause (a)
(a) Adv. to predicate of A	if	Commons	the	impeached	minister	1. a 2. favourite

Kind of Clause.	Connective.	Subject.	Adjuncts to Subject.	Predicate.	Object.	Adjuncts to Object.	Adjuncts to Predicate.
(18) A Principal	...	fact	the	is, clause (a)	...	...	...
(a) Noun completing predicate of A	that	Oxford	...	is a paradise of birds	...	...	1. almost 2. for obvious reasons
(19) A Principal	...	we	...	can pretend	to conjecture, clause (a)	...	not
(a) Noun object to 'conjecture' in A	why	artist	1. an 2. such	was selected	...	...	to deface so fine a Torso
(20) A Principal	...	he	...	must know	boundaries	its	clause (a)
(a) Adv. to predicate of A	before	man	a	begins	to make improvements on his estate	...	...

The same exercise continued in a slightly different form. The pupil is required to combine the clauses, and to place the parts of each in their most telling setting.

GENERAL ANALYSIS: OR SENTENCE PARSING FOR RELATION

21. { Principal clause: The chief influences were such
    Relative clause to 'influences': the national type of virtue had been formed by which

22. { Principal clause: I have named a number of celebrated poets
    Relative clause to 'poets': Wordsworth deserves to be placed above all of whom in my opinion

23. { Principal clause: Leeds gave all the opposition to this arrangement in public
    Relative clause to 'opposition': he could give that with decency

24. { Principal clause: A vaunting inscription had been placed over one gate
    Relative clause to 'inscription': which defied the allies to wrench from the grasp of France the prize

25. { Principal clause: Discontent and disaffection succeeded to the fervid loyalty
    Relative clause to 'loyalty': Charles had been welcomed back to Dover with which

26. { Principal clause: No abstract can give a just notion of the deep and painful interest
    Relative clause to 'interest': this book excites which

27. { Principal clause: William Mountford was the most graceful of all the actors
    Relative clause to 'actors': who were on the English stage then

28. { Principal clause: The number of cases was small
    Relative clause to 'cases': bribery was fully made out in which

29. { Principal clause: Russell remembered the reprimand still with bitterness
    Relative clause to 'reprimand': his extreme caution had drawn which upon him after the fight of Beachy Head

30. { Principal clause: The season sufficed for a short inroad and a battle
    Relative clause to 'season': the field did not require the presence of the cultivator during which

We have given a large number of sentences containing a relative clause, because this kind of clause is one of the most difficult to place.

Exercise IX

Correct the errors in the following, and give reasons for your corrections :

Few have a good word for poor Aphra, who valued qualities not usually associated with scholarship very highly. The captain took the good things which the gods provided with thankful good-humour. This lady was able to meet the man who had dared to approach her with his love without the slightest nervousness. I wrote that cruel letter to my wife, which turned her from her home, at Mrs. Gerrarde's house. He was driving away from the church where he had been married in a coach and six. The woman begged that she might have out the four shillings she had paid in bacon. Mr. Carlyle has taught us that silence is golden in thirty volumes. These twenty words translate those five which Cæsar uses, perhaps with fair accuracy. The majority of families depend on the libraries for the whole of their reading, and expect to have all the new books the moment they are published for a few guineas a year. The carriage stopped at the small gate which led by a short gravel walk to the house amidst the nods and smiles of the whole party. He always read Lord Byron's writings as soon as they were published, with great avidity. Nor, indeed, can those habits be formed with certainty which are to continue during life in a shorter space. If the Westminster Reviewer will read over what we have written twice or thrice with patience and attention, some glimpse of our meaning will break in even on his mind.

An Important Participial Construction : its Place and its Equivalents

The following examples exemplify some important uses of the participial phrase, *when the participle and the finite verb have the same subject :*

(a) '*Weakened by the anxieties of the time,* Anson fell an easy prey to cholera.'
   = (1) *Because he was weakened by the anxieties of the time,* Anson fell an easy prey to cholera.

Or :
- = (2) *Anson was weakened by the anxieties of the time,* and therefore he fell an easy prey to cholera.

(b) '*Old, broken, and wounded,* some five hundred Sepoys came to offer their services.'
- = (1) *Though they were old, broken, and wounded,* some five hundred Sepoys came to offer their services.

Or :
- = (2) *Notwithstanding that they were old, broken, and wounded,* some five hundred Sepoys came to offer their services.

(c) '*Respecting ourselves,* we shall be respected by others.'
  = *If we respect ourselves,* we shall be respected by others.

(d) '*Reaching the top of the hill,* we saw the enemy in the valley below.'
  = *When we reached the top of the hill,* we saw the enemy in the valley below.

(e) '*Scattered over the fields,* they had already begun the work of pillage.'
  = *They were scattered over the fields,* and had already begun the work of pillage.

From our examples we should learn :

1. That the participial phrase is a means of condensation ; it enables us to dispense with conjunctions and subjects.

2. That it imparts energy and animation to the sentence of which it forms a part. Notice in particular the fine suspensive effect of the phrase in its original position.

The same sentences with the participial phrases placed in other positions :

(a) 1. 'Anson, *weakened by the anxieties of the time,* fell an easy prey to cholera.'
   2. 'Anson fell an easy prey to cholera, *weakened by the anxieties of the time.*'

(b) 1. 'Some five hundred Sepoys, *old, broken, and wounded,* came to offer their services.'
   2. 'Some five hundred Sepoys came to offer their services, *old, broken, and wounded.*'

(c) 1. 'We, *respecting ourselves,* shall be respected by others.'
   2. 'We shall be respected by others, *respecting ourselves.*'

(d) 1. 'We, *reaching the top of the hill,* saw the enemy in the valley below.'
   2. 'We saw the enemy in the valley below, *reaching the top of the hill.*'

(e) 1. 'They, *scattered over the fields*, had already begun the work of pillage.'
   2. 'They had already begun the work of pillage, *scattered over the fields.*'

It is obvious that two effects follow from the placing of the phrase immediately after the subject :
1. Greater prominence is given to the subject.
2. The suspensive power of the phrase is lessened.

Notice how flat and ambiguous are the sentences in which the participial phrase is placed at the end.

The following sentences are virtually of the same type as those we have just been considering :

(a) '*Unable to reply to this argument*, the English Government yielded.'
= *Because it was unable to reply to this argument*, the English Government yielded.

Or :

= *The English Government was unable to reply to this argument*, and *therefore* it yielded.

(b) '*Habitually a hard drinker*, Walpole never became a sot.'
= *Though he was habitually a hard drinker*, Walpole never became a sot.

Or :

= *Walpole was habitually a hard drinker, but* he never became a sot.

The following is a good example of the condensed force of this participial construction :

'Betrayed, deserted, disorganised, unprovided with resources, begirt with enemies, the noble city was still no easy conquest.'
= Though betrayed, etc.

Though the species of participial phrase we are now considering is, in its function, adverbial rather than adjectival, most grammarians parse it as an adjunct to the subject.

In using this construction the young student should be careful to see that the participle has a **subject of reference.**

In each of the following examples the participle is in search of a subject :

(a) '*Writing at the close of December*, it is not possible to obtain complete statistical information for the whole year.'
(b) '*Turning then to the table of wages*, it will be easy to ascertain the labourer's position.'
(c) '*Looking out for a theme*, several crossed his mind.'

Who was writing? Who was turning? Who was looking? The subjects of the sentences are 'it' and 'several' (themes). It is plain that 'writing' and 'turning' cannot be referred to 'it,' and that 'looking' cannot be referred to 'several' (themes); and the sentences contain no other subjects to which the participles can be referred. Still greater violence is done to the sentence when the participial phrase without a subject of reference is placed at the end, as :

> 'My farm consisted of about twenty acres of excellent land, *having given a hundred pounds for my predecessor's good-will.*'

The use of the **verbal noun** also requires care. The sentence should contain the *subject* to which the action expressed by the verbal noun is intended to refer. The following example does not comply with this condition :

> 'On *reaching* the river it was found that the bridge had been carried away by the flood.'

Who or what reached the river? The sentence contains no word that properly answers to the question. Write :

> 'On reaching the river *we* (I, they) found that the bridge had been carried away by the flood.'

Exercise X

1. Condense into phrases the italicised clauses in the following :

The leaders withdrew to Trafalgar Square, and there held an orderly meeting. *The government was conscious of the necessity of settling the question,* and intended to lift it above the level of party discussion. *The Irishman was filled with a new sense of his importance,* and formed the hope of employing his influence to force hostility to England upon the American Government. *The United States Government refused to allow hostile operations against a friendly Power to be carried on along its frontier,* and took vigorous measures to suppress the outbreak. *The workmen were aware that no political change was at that time possible,* and were devoting all their attention to the tyranny of capital. *The Treaty had been made during the recess,* and therefore wanted Parliamentary ratification. *The income-tax was originally imposed as a temporary tax,* but it might now be regarded as a fixed source of income. *He ignored the successes of his opponents*, and narrated only their failures. *The prince was full of the best German traditions*, and held that the possession of the crown brought with it corresponding duties of the severest kind. *The commissioner carefully avoided the points at issue*, and declared the proceedings null and void. *Lord Raglan lost patience at the sight*, and despatched Captain Nolan with a second written order. With perfect and unswerving gallantry Lord Cardigan, *when he had placed himself at the head of the first line*, galloped against the guns. *The army had been originally despatched and equipped for a short expedition*, and had been furnished only with what was necessary for that purpose. *Lord Canning was eager to complete the suppression of the mutiny*, and urged the commander-in-chief to advance immediately into Rohilcund.

2. Expand into clauses the italicised phrases in the following, and try each phrase in another position:

Master of the road to Russia, the general had been receiving constant reinforcements. *Full of suspicion*, the Sepoys misconstrued everything. *Rudely awakened to the terrible extent of the danger*, the government exhibited the greatest energy. *Keenly alive to the advantages of direct English rule*, Lord Dalhousie lost no opportunity of asserting the power claimed by the English. *Postponed for a while by the difficulties in the Punjab*, the question of annexation came up again in 1855. Sir Henry Barnard, *weakened by his incessant exertions*, before long fell a victim to disease. *Leaving Neill to support authority in the re-occupied city*, Havelock speedily moved across the river into Oude. *Perfectly aware of the danger*, Sir Henry Lawrence used every effort to postpone the threatened outbreak. *A very gallant and energetic man*, Gubbins was wanting in breadth of view. *Afraid of any divided authority*, Lawrence insisted upon keeping the appointment of commissioner vacant. *Discovering his mistake*, the emperor cast about for means of withdrawing from his difficult position. *Absorbed in the great events going on around it, and satisfied with its own growth in material prosperity*, the nation was for a time willing to let well alone. *A self-made man*, Lincoln had forced his way, step by step, up the social scale. Another charge brought against Walpole is that, *jealous of rivals*, he surrounded himself with mediocrities.

3. Point out and correct the errors in the following:

Being early killed, I sent a party in search of his body. Gliding along the passage, many a word was uttered. Looking back, the happiness of my young life is associated with study. His career was cut short in the youth of his popularity, having been killed in a duel. Fancying that every man in office was a great man, their especial contempt was reserved for a public writer. Speaking more generally, condensation may be gained by allusions instead of expanded statements. You know that we are naturally gifted with such qualities that once placed in our right position, it is our own wilful fault if we do not maintain and improve it. Looking back upon the wonderful outcome of the idea, it seems surprising that others should not have followed up his work. Though unable to comprehend the emperor's answer, this method of escaping from his uncertainty did not occur to him. After observing the most severe caution, it is impossible to conceive a satisfactory explanation of Charles's conduct. Having perceived the weakness of his poems, they now appear to us under new titles. After fording the stream, the weather cleared. After keeping the book a month, it was returned unread. In fording the river it was found that its bed was very uneven. Weeks and months may be passed without observing a single flowering plant.

ABSOLUTE PHRASES: THEIR PLACE AND THEIR EQUIVALENTS

I. The **nominative absolute**, with its accompanying participle or participial phrase.

EXAMPLES

(a) '*The weather being fine*, the ship set sail.'

The phrase 'the weather being fine' expresses a circumstance of **cause**. Because (since, as) the weather was fine, etc.

(b) '*Our honeymoon over* (*i.e.* being over), we settled down to earnest work.'

The phrase 'our honeymoon over' expresses a circumstance of **time**. When (after) our honeymoon was over, etc.

(c) 'They crept and crept, *the hem of her dress just touching his gaiter.*'

The absolute phrase here expresses the circumstances that accompanied their creeping. It vaguely denotes the **manner** of their creeping.

(d) '*Given fair weather* (=fair weather being given), we shall reach home to-morrow.'
= If fair weather be given, etc.

The absolute phrase here denotes **condition.**

From these examples it is obvious that this species of absolute phrase is adverbial in function. Its position is sometimes *before* and sometimes *after* what it qualifies. See the examples in the exercises below.

II. The **absolute infinitive,** sometimes called the Parenthetical Infinitive.

EXAMPLES

(a) '*To confess the truth*, this man is a rascal.'
= *The truth being confessed*, etc. *If the truth must be confessed*, etc.
(b) '*Not to mince matters*, the boy is a thief.'

This kind of absolute phrase denotes **purpose, time,** etc. The position of this phrase is at the head of the sentence.

III. **Except,** with the noun, phrase, or sentence governed by it.

EXAMPLES

(a) 'All the passengers were saved *except five*' (=*five being excepted*, or *if we except five*).
(b) 'There was nothing to be done *except to proceed with the attainder*' (=*to proceed with the attainder being excepted*, or *if we except to proceed*, etc.)
(c) 'Of Livingstone's early boyhood there is little to be said *except that he was a favourite at home*' (=*that he was a favourite being excepted*, or *if we except that he was*, etc.)
(d) 'There was nothing left *but* (except) *to meet defiance by defiance*' (=*to meet defiance by defiance being excepted*, or *if we except*, etc.)

This phrase is usually placed at the end of the sentence.

(*Note.—But* is frequently used for *except.*)

We have treated the construction with 'except' and 'but' as adverbial. It is, however, by some regarded as adjectival. In this case the phrases should be regarded as limiting 'passengers' (a), 'nothing' (b), 'little' (c), and 'nothing' (d) respectively. But whether we regard this construction as adverbial or as adjectival, its place in the sentence is the same.

EXERCISE XI

1. Notice the position of, and parse the italicised phrases in the following :

Thus reasoned they in the emperor's cabinet, *their eyes on the map and compass in hand*. *The effort to recall the dream having failed,* make an experiment. *The rain having completely passed and the sky cleared,* I expressed a wish for some fresh air. The woman speaks and the men listen to her, *no need for concealing or enslaving her*. *The marriage being once decided on,* Mary could think of nothing else. Tess and the other three were dressing themselves rapidly, *the whole bevy having agreed to go to church.* *The facts once classified, once understood,* the judgment based upon them ought to be independent of the individual mind which examines them. Searching for the plant was a most tedious business, *not more than half a dozen shoots of it being discernible in the whole field.* (Transpose 'it' and 'plant,' and place the absolute phrase at the head of the sentence.) *The rain having passed,* the uplands were dry. Meanwhile his companions, who were left behind in the tavern, *the second flight coming so close upon the first,* looked blankly in each other's faces. England sustained a great loss this week, *Tennyson having passed away on the morning of Thursday*. *Every window of the house being open,* Clare could hear across the yard each trivial sound of the retiring household. None *but the brave* deserves the fair. Do we find here nothing *but fairyland?* Nothing remained to be done *except to sign the agreement.* This poem is full of delicate loves, noble sorrows, lofty ideas, where no voice is heard *except that of thinkers and poets.* Tennyson has succeeded in seizing beauty in its fulness, because he cared for nothing *but beauty.* In the nineteen propositions we see little to blame *except the articles against the Catholics.*

2. Expand into their equivalent clauses the italicised phrases in the foregoing exercise.

3. Compose a dozen sentences of the type of those in 1 above.

PART III

THE COMPOUND SENTENCE

A SENTENCE consisting of two or more clauses that are grammatically independent of each other is called a **compound sentence**. In the compound sentence independent clauses are placed side by side either for the purpose of *adding*, or for the purpose of *opposing* or *contrasting* what the clauses express. Clauses so placed are called **co-ordinate clauses** or **co-ordinate sentences**; that is, they are considered as of equal rank.

I. The addition of what the clauses express: the **copulative** or **cumulative relation**.

EXAMPLES

(a) 'The minister was waylaid by a gang of bullies, and his nose was cut to the bone.'

The clauses are here connected by the conjunction 'and,' the chief of the copulative or cumulative conjunctions.

(b) 'The king then read the letters, divided them into packets, and signified his pleasure by two or three words.'

In a compound sentence of three members the 'and' is usually omitted from the second member. This is a favourite type of sentence.

(c) 'Without valour none could then be eminent, few could be secure.'
(d) 'I came, I saw, I conquered.'
(e) 'Life passes, riches fly away, popularity is fickle, the senses decay, the world changes, friends die.'

Clauses placed side by side without the copulative conjunction, as in (c), (d), (e), are called **collateral** clauses. The relation is cumulative. Notice the fine effect of the ellipsis of the conjunction.

(f) 'The troops had never fought so well, nor had the genius of their chief ever been so conspicuous.'

Here 'nor' = 'and not,' and the relation is cumulative. Notice how 'nor' attracts the verb.

(g) 'He was diligent, therefore he succeeded.'

The word 'therefore' is strictly an adverb and does not join the clauses, which may be regarded as collateral, the conjunction 'and' being understood. When the second clause states a result or consequence of the first clause, it is sometimes said to be in *illative* (inferential) relation to the first. The relation is really cumulative, like that of the other examples.

(h) 1. 'Man is man and master of his fate.'
2. 'The water is nought and the ground barren.'

Here 'and' = 'and therefore,' 'and consequently.'

(i) 'I am a true Englishman; I felt to the quick for the disgrace of England.'
= I am a true Englishman, *and therefore* I felt, etc.

The second clause states a consequence of the first, and the ellipsis of 'and therefore' makes the statement specially energetic.

II. The opposition or contrast of what the clauses express: the **disjunctive relation**.

EXAMPLES

(a) 'Either you must get another watch, or I must get another secretary.'

The one statement is *opposed* to the other. This is sometimes called the **alternative relation**, because there is a choice between two statements.

(b) 'John was brave, but James was a coward.'

Here the character of John is contrasted with that of James.

The sense of the one clause is contrasted with that of the other. Such clauses are sometimes said to be in **adversative relation.**

(c) 'Elizabeth's aversion to the Puritans was political; James's was personal.'
= Elizabeth's aversion to the Puritans was political, *but* James's was personal.

The ellipsis of the conjunction adds energy to the contrast.

(d) 'The triumph of the navy added nothing to Cromwell's fame, its increase nothing to his means of overawing his enemies, its leader was not his friend; yet he took a peculiar pleasure in encouraging that noble service.'

The first three clauses are in cumulative relation, and seem to point to the consequence that Cromwell took no pleasure in the naval service of England. From this conclusion the mind of the reader is arrested by 'yet,' which is followed by the statement of a consequence wholly opposed to the natural inference from the three preceding clauses.

'But,' 'still,' 'but still,' 'but then,' 'nevertheless,' have a similar *arrestive* force. Find examples in your reading-book.

The clauses of the compound sentence frequently have parts in common.

EXAMPLES

(a) 'The two men shook hands and departed.'
= The two men shook hands and the two men (they) departed.

The subject 'the two men' is common to the two clauses. This community of subject may be shown thus:

$$\text{The two men} \begin{cases} \text{shook hands} \\ \text{and} \\ \text{departed.} \end{cases}$$

(b) 'We neither adopt nor condemn the language which the great orator employs.'
= We do not adopt the language which the great orator employs, and we do not condemn the language which the great orator employs.

The subject 'we' and also the object 'the language,' etc., are common to the two statements.

The community of subject and object may be shown thus:

We { neither adopt / nor condemn } the language which the great orator employs.

(c) 'Danby knew the English people and the House of Commons.'
= Danby knew the English people and Danby (he) knew the House of Commons.

The subject 'Danby' and the predicate 'knew' are common to the two statements. The community of subject and predicate may be exhibited thus:

$$\text{Danby} \left\{ \text{knew} \right\} \begin{array}{c} \text{the English people} \\ \text{and} \\ \text{the House of Commons.} \end{array}$$

(d) 'The soldiers advanced and retired in good order.'
= The soldiers advanced in good order and the soldiers (they) retired in good order.

The subject 'the soldiers' and the adverbial adjunct 'in good order' are common to the two statements.
This community may be exhibited thus:

$$\text{The soldiers} \left\{ \begin{array}{c} \text{advanced} \\ \text{and} \\ \text{retired} \end{array} \right\} \text{in good order.}$$

(e) 'The Popish Plot, the murder of Godfrey, the infamous inventions of Oates, the discovery of Colman's letters, had excited the nation to madness.'

This is a simple sentence with a compound subject.

The Popish Plot
The murder of Godfrey
The infamous inventions of Oates
The discovery of Colman's letters
} had excited the nation to madness.

(f) 'Spain and the Empire were in arms.'

Here the form of the verb shows that 'Spain' and 'the Empire' together form the subject of the sentence. The sentence is simple and the subject compound. If we resolve the sentence we must change the verb, thus:

Spain *was* in arms
and
the Empire *was* in arms.

This is, of course, quite unnecessary. We must recognise

the fact that *the co-ordinating conjunctions sometimes join parts of sentences.*

OTHER EXAMPLES

(a) 'A tyrant trampled on the liberties and religion of the realm.'

A tyrant trampled on the $\left\{\begin{array}{c}\text{liberties}\\ \text{and}\\ \text{religion}\end{array}\right\}$ of the realm.

'And' here joins two nouns.

(b) 'Essex added a yet sadder and more painful story to the bloody chronicles of the Tower.'

Essex added a yet $\left\{\begin{array}{c}\text{sadder}\\ \text{and}\\ \text{more painful}\end{array}\right\}$ story to the bloody chronicles of the Tower.

'And' here joins two adjectives.

(c) 'I will vex you with none of these well-meant but wearisome little falsehoods.'

I will vex you with none of these $\left\{\begin{array}{c}\text{well-meant}\\ \text{but}\\ \text{wearisome}\end{array}\right\}$ little falsehoods.

'But' here contrasts two adjuncts.

(d) 'Temple resolved to be safe, to enjoy himself, and to let the world take its course.'

Temple resolved $\left\{\begin{array}{l}\text{to be safe (and)}\\ \text{to enjoy himself}\\ \text{and}\\ \text{to let the world take its course.}\end{array}\right.$

The object is compound, its members being joined by 'and.'

(e) 'We know nothing either of the diseases or of the remedies of the Druids.'

We know nothing $\left\{\begin{array}{c}\text{either of the diseases}\\ \text{or of the remedies}\end{array}\right\}$ of the Druids.

The double conjunction 'either—or' joins alternatively the phrases 'of the diseases (of the Druids)' and 'of the remedies (of the Druids).' We may, of course, resolve the sentence thus :

    A. We know nothing of the diseases (of the Druids),
    B. and we know nothing of the remedies of the Druids.

But such a resolution is hardly more necessary than is the resolution of 'He was promoted deservedly' into 'He was promoted and deserved it.'

(*f*) 'Halifax wanted neither arguments nor eloquence.'

Halifax wanted { neither arguments
nor eloquence.

Here the function of the double conjunction 'neither—nor' is to exclude both 'arguments' and 'eloquence.' We may resolve the sentence thus:

    A. Halifax did not want arguments,
    B. and Halifax did not want eloquence.

The resolution may help us to understand, but it does not help us to construct the sentence.

(*g*) 'The choice lay, not between Cromwell and liberty, but between Cromwell and the Stuarts.'

'Not—but' may be regarded as a double conjunction, the function of which is to exclude one thing to bring another into prominence. In the example 'not' excludes the adverbial adjunct 'between Cromwell and liberty,' and in this way assists 'but' to bring into prominence the adverbial adjunct 'between Cromwell and the Stuarts.' We may resolve the sentence thus:

    A. The choice lay not between Cromwell and liberty,
    B. but the choice lay between Cromwell and the Stuarts.

This sentence shows that 'and' may join two nouns; it also shows the proper use of the preposition 'between.'

(*h*) 'He thought himself necessary both to the Parliament and to the army.'

'Both—and' is a double conjunction, the function of which is to put special emphasis on the combination of the phrases 'to the Parliament' and 'to the army.' The sentence is simple.

He thought himself necessary { both to the Parliament
and to the army.

(*i*) 'Tennyson's ideal of spiritual life included not only the individual, but the nation.'

Tennyson's ideal of spiritual life included { not only the individual,
but the nation.

H

The function of the couple (or double conjunction) 'not only—but' is to emphasise the second of two circumstances by calling attention to the fact that the first does not stand alone.

'Not only—but also' makes the second circumstance still more emphatic.

It is important to note that each member of the couples 'either—or,' 'neither—nor,' 'not—but,' 'both—and,' 'not only—but,' 'not only—but also,' should be followed by the same part of speech. See examples (d), (e), (f), (g), (h).

Examples of Errors in the Use of these Couples

(a) 'He has been either educated at home or at a private school.'

'Either—or' is intended to oppose alternatively the phrases 'at home' and 'at a private school.' The sentence should read:
 'He has been educated either at home or at a private school.'

(b) 'He has been neither educated at home nor at a private school.'

'Neither—nor' is intended to exclude both alternatives 'at home' and 'at a private school.' The sentence should therefore read:
 'He has been educated neither at home nor at a private school.'

(c) 'He was not honoured with this reward, but with the approbation of the people.'

The circumstance intended to be excluded is, not 'honoured,' but 'with this reward.' The sentence should therefore read:

'He was honoured, not with this reward, but with the approbation of the people.'

(d) 'The man of good birth may not only lack money, but good health.'

'Good health' is intended to be emphatically connected with 'money.' The writer has connected it with 'lack.' The sentence should read:

'The man of good birth may lack not only money, but good health.'

Froude has the following construction of this couple:

'Traces, not of her participation only, but of her own originating hand, were visible in every trouble which had distracted Scotland.'

Note the position of 'only' in this sentence.

The following fine sentence is from the pen of the same writer:

'The petition claims especial notice not only because it was the first movement towards a separation from Rome, but because it originated, not with the king, not with the Parliament, not with the people, but with a section of the clergy themselves.'

Notice the setting of the couples and the fine suspensive effect of the repetition of the exclusive 'not.'

When 'neither—nor' is intended to exclude more than two things or circumstances, 'nor' must be repeated, as:

'She shall rule neither my thoughts, nor my words, nor my actions.'

The couple 'either—or' may indicate a choice of one of several things or circumstances. In this case 'or' must be repeated, as:

'William required Harold either to resign the kingdom, or to hold it of him in fealty, or to submit their cause to the arbitration of the pope, or to fight him in single combat.'

EXAMPLES OF COMMON ERRORS IN THE CONTRACTED COMPOUND SENTENCE

(a) 'His diet was simple, and his prayers long and fervent.'

The contraction is in the predicate.
The sentence resolved:

> A. His diet was simple
> and
> B. his prayers *was* long and fervent.

The copula verb 'was' agrees in number with the subject of the first clause, but not with that of the second. The contraction therefore involves a violation of the rule: that a plural subject requires a plural verb. The sentence should read:

'His diet was simple, and his prayers were long and fervent.'

(b) 'My intentions were good, but my perseverance faulty.'

The common part is 'were.' Resolve the sentence:

  A. My intentions were good
    but
  B. my perseverance *were* faulty.

The resolution makes the error obvious: the singular subject has a plural verb. The subjects of the compound sentence differ in number, and therefore cannot stand in the same relation to the common part.

Exercise I

Correct the following, and give reasons for your corrections:

The authorities should not blame the system, but their own want of judgment. The real danger to the discipline of the army does not lie within, but without the service. A punishment not inflicted by a general rule but by an arbitrary discretion, cannot serve the purpose of a warning. It is not the business of such a body to check, but to act. Whatever of political freedom either exists in Europe or in America, has sprung from those institutions. I neither spoke to him nor to his brother. This does not mean either security for the ministers or their policy. We are not much in the habit of either idolising the living or the dead. Johnson had not studied the genus man, but the genus Londoner. I am neither an ascetic in theory or practice. He is neither disposed to sanction bloodshed nor deceit. We cannot admit that either in qualities of heart or head, his women are inferior to the women we generally meet. These tales will not merely interest children, but grown-up persons. Homer was not only the maker of a nation, but of a language. Every composition is fairly liable to criticism, both in regard to its design and to its execution. Great was the generalship and various the contrivances. His brow was wrinkled, his lip compressed, his eyes full of a strong calm. His kindness of heart was great, and his acquirements considerable. The country was divided into counties, and the counties placed under magistrates. He belongs to one class, and the hewers of wood and the drawers of water to another. We may not suffer from work itself, but from want of work. There was neither time for remonstrance, nor remedy.

The COMPOUND SUBORDINATE CLAUSE

I. The Noun Clause.

EXAMPLES

(a) 'Hastings and his counsel desired that the managers should open all the charges and produce all the evidence.'

Hastings and his counsel desired } that { the managers should open all the charges
and
the managers should produce all the evidence.

The clauses following 'that' form a compound noun clause. The contractions in the compound clause may be exhibited thus :

That the managers should { open all the charges
and
produce all the evidence.

There is entire community of conjunction and subject, and partial community of predicate.

(b) 'Hastings knew that the favour of his employers depended chiefly on their dividends, and that their dividends depended chiefly on the investment.'

Hastings knew { that the favour of his employers depended chiefly on their dividends
and
that their dividends depended chiefly on the investment.

The noun clause is compound and uncontracted. When, as here, the verbs of all the clauses are in the same mood and tense, the ellipsis of the second 'that' is apt to cause ambiguity, an ambiguity often met with.

'Hastings knew that the favour of his employers depended chiefly on their dividends, and their dividends depended chiefly on the investment.'

With the ellipsis of 'that' the last clause might be taken by the reader to be co-ordinate, not with the noun clause, but with the principal.

II. The **Relative Clause**.

(c) 'The reappearance of a man who had been among the most distinguished of a generation that had passed away, who now belonged to history, and who seemed to have risen from the dead, could not but produce a solemn and pathetic effect.'

The reappearance of a man { who had been among the most distinguished of a generation that had passed away, who now belonged to history, and who seemed to have risen from the dead, } { could not but produce a solemn and pathetic effect. }

The relative clause is compound and uncontracted. As a rule, the *relative should be repeated* when it is the subject of several verbs. It may, however, be omitted if its omission does not produce ambiguity, as :

(1) 'We find in the existing schools an education for our children which meets our wants and *is not beyond our means.*'
(2) 'Many devices which now mitigate the heat of the climate, *preserve health, and prolong life,* were then unknown.'

In each of the sentences the relative clause is compound and contracted. We may exhibit the clauses thus :

(1) which { meets our wants and is not beyond our means. }

(2) which now { mitigate the heat of the climate, preserve health, and prolong life. }

EXAMPLES OF ERRORS IN THE COMPOUND RELATIVE CLAUSE

(1) 'He lives in the upper part of the house, of which I know nothing and have never seen.'

As the compound relative clause stands, 'of which I' is the common part. Resolve the clause thus :

   A. of which I know nothing
           and
   B. *of which* I have never seen.

The resolution shows that in the second clause 'which' should be governed, not by 'of,' but by 'have seen.' The sentence should read :

'He lives in the upper part of the house, of which I know nothing and which I have never seen.'

(2) 'I do not know out of Cambridge any one with whom I can converse more pleasantly or would prefer as my companion.'

As the compound relative clause stands, the common part is 'with whom I.' Resolve the clause:

    A. with whom I can converse more pleasantly,
                    or
    B. *with whom* I would prefer as my companion.

The resolution discloses the error: the relative in the second clause requires to be under the government, not of 'with,' but of 'would prefer.' The sentence should read:

'I do not know out of Cambridge any one with whom I can converse more pleasantly, or whom I would prefer as a companion.'

III. The **Adverbial Clause.**

(d) 'When Hastings had passed many years in retirement, and had long outlived the common age of men, he again became for a short time an object of general attention.'

The common part of the compound adverbial clause may be exhibited thus:

When Hastings { had passed many years in retirement
                  and
                had long outlived the common age of men.

Or thus (further contracted):

When Hastings had { passed many years in retirement
                    and
                     long outlived the common age of men.

(e) 'Even to the present day Cromwell's character, though constantly attacked and scarcely ever defended, is popular with the great body of our countrymen.'

The following expansion of the compound adverbial clause exhibits the common part:

Though it is { constantly attacked
               and
              scarcely ever defended.

The resolution of the clause:

A. Though it is constantly attacked
and
B. though it is scarcely ever defended.

The following examples exemplify types of errors that are not uncommon:

(a) 'The journey must remain fixed for the latter end of April, *unless* any very bad weather should set in, or *that* you can arrange with agreeable travelling company.'

The clauses of the compound adverbial clause should be introduced by the same conjunction either expressed or understood. 'That' should therefore be 'unless.'

(b) 'I never have, and never will, attack a man for his opinions.'

$$\text{I never} \begin{cases} \text{have } attack \\ \text{and} \\ \text{will attack} \end{cases} \text{a man for his opinions.}$$

The auxiliary 'have' should be followed by the past participle and the auxiliary 'will' by the infinitive, of the principal verb: when the clauses of a compound sentence contain auxiliaries that take after them different forms of the principal verb, the ellipsis of the principal verb is not justifiable. The sentence should read:

'I never have attacked, and never will attack, a man for his opinions.'

(c) 'I have no more to add, and believe me to remain yours, etc.'

The parts joined by a co-ordinating conjunction must stand in the same relation to the common part (Bain).

The form of this sentence makes 'I' the common part.

A. I have no more to add
and
B. (I) believe me to remain yours, etc.

It is obvious from the resolution that the two clauses have not the same subject. The error involved in the sentence may be shown in another way.

The verb of the first clause is in the indicative mood, that of the second clause is in the imperative mood; the co-ordinating conjunctions, as a rule, join the *same moods* as well as the *same tenses* of verbs; hence 'and' is here improperly employed. The sentence may be amended thus:

'I have no more to add, and desire you to believe me to remain yours, etc.'

(d) 'Did ever man put God to the proof on that promise, and found it broken?'

In each clause the mood of the verb is indicative and the tense past; but in the first clause we have the interrogative form and in the second the affirmative form, of the past indicative. The constructions are *mixed*. The sentence is compound, and the common part is 'Did ever man.'

Did ever man $\begin{cases} \text{put God to the proof on that promise} \\ \text{and} \\ \textit{find}\text{ it broken?} \end{cases}$

Exercise II

Correct the following, and give reasons for your corrections:

Originality in politics consists in the use and application of the ideas which we get or are given to us. One of the last of his speeches was delivered in defence of Warren Hastings, with whom he was on terms of intimate friendship, and regarded as the saviour of India. If I do not speak of them, it is because they do not come within my subject, and not that they are lightly esteemed by me. If you had a niece engaged to be married, and that you thought the match a good one, how would you like to see it broken off? Far distant be the day when the measured walk takes the place of the manly exercise of the cricket ground, or that lectures multiply while sports decrease. I tell him that if you were to hear him speak English, that you could not refrain from kissing him. We are apt to imagine that what is, always has, and always will be. You will bear this as you have so many things. I am anxious for the time when he will talk as much nonsense to me as I have to him. He ridicules the notion that truth will prevail; it never has and it never will. Blake wrote and drew with marvellous genius, but I doubt whether any one has or would care to follow in his steps. My own impression about it was that the Reformation was both a good thing and that in England it had been accomplished with peculiar skill and success. We may not only fairly assume that Shelley learnt much from Godwin, but also that his whole course of thought was guided by this.

Mixed Sentences

The typical English sentence is neither simply compound nor simply complex; it is both *compound* and *complex*.

EXAMPLES

(a) 'The old subjects of contention had vanished, and those which were to succeed had not yet appeared.'

Analysis (*Note:* The principal clauses are denoted by the capitals):

```
    A. The old subject of contention had vanished .      simple
           and
    B. those had not yet appeared ⎫
       |                          ⎬  .  .  .  complex
Rel. cl. : which were to succeed  ⎭
```

The sentence is compound, its first member being simple and its second member complex.

(b) 'The boats plied busily; company after company was quickly landed; and, as soon as the men touched the shore, they swarmed up the steep ascent with great alacrity.'

Analysis :

```
    A. The boats plied busily    .    .    .    .   simple

    B. company after company was quickly landed    simple
           and
    C. they swarmed up the steep ascent         ⎫
              with great alacrity               ⎬  . complex
           |                                    ⎭
Ad. cl. of time : as soon as the men touched the shore
```

The sentence consists of two simple members 'A' and 'B' and one complex member 'C.' The compound sentence having its last member complex is a very common cast of sentence.

(c) 'Not fifteen minutes had elapsed since Montcalm had first moved on his line of battle, and already all was lost.'

THE COMPOUND SENTENCE

Analysis:

$$\left.\begin{array}{l}\text{A. Not fifteen minutes had elapsed}\\ \overline{\text{Ad. cl of time: since Montcalm had moved on his}}\\ \qquad\qquad\qquad\text{line of battle}\end{array}\right\} \quad \text{complex}$$

and

B. already all was lost . . . .   simple

Here the first member of the compound sentence is complex and the last simple.

(d) 'The postman who brings my letters walks eight thousand miles a year, and enjoys the most perfect regularity of health.'

This sentence is of the same cast as (c).

(e) 'We have done those things which we ought not to have done; we have left undone those things which we ought to have done, and there is no health in us.'

Analysis:

$$\left.\begin{array}{l}\text{A. We have done those things}\\ \overline{\text{Rel. cl.: which we ought not to have done}}\end{array}\right\} \quad \text{complex}$$

$$\left.\begin{array}{l}\text{B. we have left undone those things}\\ \overline{\text{Rel. cl.: which we ought to have done}}\end{array}\right\} \quad \text{complex}$$

and

C. there is no health in us . . . .   simple

The first two members of the compound sentence are complex, and the last is simple.

(f) 'The pigeons began to move off in a direction quite different from that in which they had arrived the evening before, and at sunrise all that were able to fly had disappeared.'

Analysis:

$$\left.\begin{array}{l}\text{A. The pigeons began to move off in a direction}\\ \quad\text{quite different from that}\\ \overline{\text{Rel. cl.: in which they had arrived the evening before}}\end{array}\right\} \quad \text{complex}$$

and

$$\left.\begin{array}{l}\text{B. at sunrise all had disappeared}\\ \overline{\text{Rel. cl.: that were able to fly}}\end{array}\right\} \quad \text{complex}$$

The sentence is compound, and each of its members is complex.

The compound sentence is sometimes both complex and contracted, as:

(*g*) 'The soldier claims, and is granted, the consideration which accrues to members of an honourable service, and the respect which men of character are never slow to render.'

The sentence resolved:

A. The soldier claims the consideration which accrues to members of an honourable service, and the respect which men of character are never slow to render (complex),

and

B. (The soldier) is granted the consideration which accrues to members of an honourable service, and the respect which men of character are never slow to render (complex).

The resolution shows that the sentence is much contracted in subject and object. The community of subject and object may be shown thus:

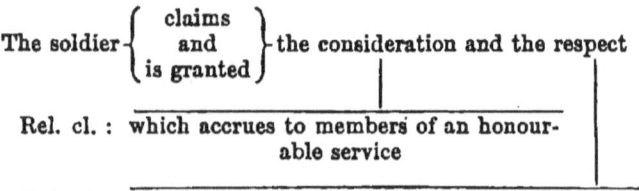

Rel. cl. : which accrues to members of an honourable service

Rel. cl. : which men of character are never slow to render

Exercise III

Select from your reading-book sentences of the same cast as those given above, and give their general analysis.

(*Note*.—Uncontracted principal clauses not joined by 'and,' and principal clauses in adversative relation are generally separated by a semicolon.)

PART IV

ANALYSIS OF COMPLEX SENTENCES OF MORE THAN TWO CLAUSES

EXAMPLES

(a) 'What these reflections were, and whether they were reflections of which he had a right to complain, we have now no means of deciding.'

Analysis (or sentence parsing for relation and position):

Principal clause: We have now no means of deciding
Compound noun clause to 'deciding'
{ what these reflections were
  and
  whether they were reflections }
Relative clause to 'reflections' in the second noun clause: of which he had no right to complain.

Or, denoting the principal clause by A, we may show the relation of the clauses thus:

A. We have now no means of deciding { what these reflections were
  and
  whether they were reflections } Compound noun clause

Rel. cl.: of which he had no right to complain

The sentence is skilfully constructed. The writer wishes to direct special attention to the noun clauses; he therefore places them before their governing clause. This arrangement also makes the suspense of the sentence perfect.

Variation:

'We have now no means of deciding what these reflections were, and whether they were reflections of which he had a right to complain.'

Decidedly inferior to the original arrangement.

(*b*) '"Those legal checks which, while the sovereign remained dependent on his subjects, had been adequate to the purpose for which they were designed, were now found wanting."'

Analysis:

Principal clause: Those legal checks were now found wanting
Relative clause to 'checks': which had been adequate to the purpose
Relative clause to 'purpose': for which they were designed
Adverbial clause of time to the first relative clause: while the sovereign remained dependent on his subjects.

Notice how all the subordinate clauses are dovetailed into the principal clause, and how the time clause is dovetailed into the clause it qualifies. The sentence is a model of clause setting, and its suspense is perfect.

Variations:

1. 'Those legal checks which had, while the sovereign remained dependent on his subjects, been adequate to the purpose for which they were designed, were now found wanting.'

The adverbial clause is placed within the predicate instead of immediately after the connective of the clause it is intended to qualify. This is an effective variation.

2. 'Those legal checks which had been adequate to the purpose for which they were designed while the sovereign remained dependent on his subjects, were now found wanting.'

In its present situation the time clause bears, not on 'which had been adequate to the purpose,' but on 'for which they were designed.' This variation does not give the sense intended by the writer; it is, therefore, inadmissible.

Exercise I

1. Analyse the following sentences, and point out their merits or their defects; also give what variations you think worth giving, and point out the merits or the defects of such variations:

ANALYSIS OF COMPLEX SENTENCES

(1) If the admiral and his officers had perceived that they were marked men, they might in self-defence have become traitors.

(2) The alliance against Holland, formidable as it was, was yet of such a nature that it could not succeed at all unless it succeeded at once.

(3) The Triple Alliance only compelled Lewis to make peace on the terms on which, before the alliance was formed, he had offered to make peace.

(4) When at last the constancy of the lovers had triumphed over all the obstacles which kinsmen and rivals could oppose to their union, a yet more serious difficulty befell them.

(5) Poor Mistress Osborne fell ill of small-pox, and, though she escaped with life, lost all her beauty.

(6) We know on the best evidence that, before Byron published these lines, he was greatly elated by the compliments paid to his maiden speech in the House of Lords.

(7) Those who disliked the Master of Stair did him the justice to own that, where his schemes of policy were not concerned, he was a very good-natured man.

(8) Hastings argued that, if the English force was withdrawn, Oude would certainly become a prey to anarchy, and would probably be overrun by a Mahratta army.

(9) If men are to wait for liberty till they become wise and good in slavery, they may indeed wait for ever.

(10) Till he had a wife he could do nothing; and, when he had a wife, he did whatever she chose.

(11) The only party against whom nothing could be produced was the party who, in respect of blood, had the weakest claim of all.

(12) 'I have become French,' said the queen, 'but I will show my enemies that I can be Spanish when occasion demands it.'

(13) Fitzgerald, as soon as the army was landed, retired into the interior; but, finding that the deputy lay idle within the walls, he recovered heart.

(14) Davison might have taken a terrible revenge upon the queen if he had explained the meaning of these words; but what he told the privy council he concealed from the world.

(15) So eager was the queen that her story should be believed, that nothing so much pleased her as an indication that credit was attached to it.

2. Treat in the same manner the sentences selected by the teacher from your reading-book.

Synthesis of Complex Sentences of more than Two Clauses

Examples

Analysis:

(a)

    Principal clause: A river lay before Clive
    Relative clause to 'river': not one of his little band would ever return over which
    Adverbial clause of condition: if things went ill.

Synthesis:

    'Before Clive lay a river over which, if things went ill, not one of his little band would ever return.'

Notice (1) the inversion of the principal clause and the purpose of it, viz. to bring into proximity the relative and its antecedent, and (2) the position of the adverbial clause. The conditional clause is usually placed before the clause it qualifies; but, as no clause may be placed between the relative and its antecedent, it is clear that an adverbial clause that qualifies a relative clause cannot precede the relative pronoun; in this case its usual placement is immediately after the relative. In its present form the sentence is periodic; in the following form it is loose.

    'Before Clive lay a river over which not one of his little band would ever return, if things went ill.'

Analysis:

(b)

    Principal clause: They came on manfully
    Adverbial clause of concession to 'came': though the assailants had lost all the advantage
    Relative clause to 'advantage': which belongs to a surprise.

Synthesis:

    'Though the assailants had lost all the advantage which belongs to a surprise, they came on manfully.'

ANALYSIS OF COMPLEX SENTENCES

The concessive clause is, in accordance with the general rule, placed before the clause it qualifies, the relative clause falls naturally into its proper place immediately after the antecedent noun, and the principal clause is placed at the end. In this form the sentence is periodic ; in the following form it is loose :

> 'The assailants came on manfully, though they had lost all the advantage which belongs to a surprise.'

In the loose sentence notice the transposition of the noun and pronoun and the purpose of it.

Analysis :

(c)

Principal clause : After tea my aunt suggested
Noun clause to 'suggested': that we should take a little walk up the village
Adverbial clause of cause to 'should take': as (=since) the evening was perfectly fine.

Synthesis :

> 'After tea my aunt suggested that, as the evening was perfectly fine, we should take a little walk up the village.'

In accordance with the general rule, the conjunction introducing the noun clause follows the governing clause ; then comes the adverbial clause, and after it the noun clause which it qualifies. This is the usual order in sentences of this type. An adverbial clause that is intended to qualify a noun clause should not be placed before the introductory conjunction of the noun clause. As the sentence now stands it is periodic ; if we place the adverbial clause after the clause it qualifies we cast the sentence loose, thus :

> 'After tea my aunt suggested that we should take a little walk up the village, as the evening was perfectly fine.'

In the following sentence the conditional clause is faultily placed :

> 'If Faulkland had lived through the scenes that followed, we have little doubt that he would have condemned himself to share the exile and beggary of the royal family.'

The conditional clause is intended to qualify the noun

clause. In its present position it ought to be regarded as bearing on the principal clause. Read:

> 'We have little doubt that, if Faulkland had lived through the scenes that followed, he would have condemned himself to share the exile and beggary of the royal family.'

Or:

> 'We have little doubt that Faulkland, if he had lived through the scenes that followed, would have condemned himself,' etc.

OTHER EXAMPLES OF THE SAME TYPE AS (c)

(1) 'The Queen of Scots determined that, if die she must, she would give her death the character of a martyrdom.'

Notice the very effective partial inversion in the conditional clause.

The same sentence cast loose and without the inversion:

> 'The Queen of Scots determined that she would give her death the character of a martyrdom, if she must die.'

(2) 'It is a curious fact that, when I return from Switzerland, I am unable to discover in our English midlands anything but a dead level of fertile plains.'

(3) 'Mr. Welldon pointed out that, unless a boy understood something of English grammar, the difficulty of translating correctly into Latin must be greatly increased.'

The points to be noted in these three sentences are the placement of the adverbial clause and how this placement affects the sentences. Cast Nos. 2 and 3 loose and observe the effect. In all the preceding sentences compare the 'draggle' of the loose with the sprightly energy of the periodic structure.

Owing to the ambiguity lurking in the pronoun 'it,' the following sentence is better in the loose than in the periodic form:

> 'Her hand was so severely injured that, unless she had the forefinger amputated, she would entirely lose the use of it.'

The pronoun 'it' is intended to refer to 'hand'; owing to its placement, however, it ought to be referred to 'forefinger.' This reference would obviously make nonsense. 'Hand' should be repeated or the sentence cast loose thus:

'Her hand was so severely injured that she would entirely lose the use of it, unless she had the forefinger amputated.'

Analysis:

(d)

Principal clause : The French admiral would have been in Leith
Adverbial clause of condition to pred. of prin. cl. : had the weather been fair
Adverbial clause of time to pred. of prin. cl. : before the English fleet had cleared the Thames.

Synthesis :

'Had the weather been fair, the French admiral would have been in Leith before the English fleet had cleared the Thames.'

The principal clause is qualified by two adverbial clauses, one of which is placed before and the other after it. This is in accordance with the general rule of distribution of such adjuncts. The conditional clause naturally occupies the position of emphasis at the head of the sentence. The sentence cast loose :

'The French admiral would have been in Leith before the English fleet had cleared the Thames, had the weather been fair' (or, if the weather had been fair).

Compare the following variations with the original form of the sentence :

(1) 'Before the English fleet had cleared the Thames, the French admiral, had the weather been fair, would have been in Leith.'

(2) 'The French admiral, had the weather been fair, would have been in Leith before the English fleet had cleared the Thames.'

Analysis:

(e)

Principal clause : The angry passions had fixed themselves in the form of deep and lasting hatred
Relative clause to 'passions': which would have died away almost as soon
Adverbial clause of degree to 'soon': as they appeared
Adverbial clause of condition to pred. of rel. cl. : if the contest had been short.

Synthesis:

'The angry passions which, if the contest had been short, would have died away almost as soon as they appeared, had fixed themselves in the form of deep and lasting hatred.'

If we regard 'as soon as' as a compound conjunction, the clause introduced by it is a *time* clause, and the adverb 'almost' qualifies the time clause. For the position of the conditional clause see the note on sentence (*a*).

Analysis:

(*f*)

Principal clause: We doubt greatly
Noun clause to 'doubt': whether Mr. Southey's poems will be read fifty years hence } Complex

but

Principal clause: we have no doubt whatever
Noun clause in apposition to 'doubt': that they will be admired
Adverbial clause of condition to noun cl.: if they are read. } Complex

The sentence is compound and each of its members is complex.

Synthesis:

'We doubt greatly whether Mr. Southey's poems will be read fifty years hence; but we have no doubt whatever that, if they are read, they will be admired.'

Variations:

(1) 'We greatly doubt whether Mr. Southey's poems will be read fifty years hence; but that, if they are read, they will be admired, we have no doubt whatever.'

(2) 'Whether Mr. Southey's poems will be read fifty years hence, we greatly doubt; but that, if they are read, they will be admired, we have no doubt whatever.'

(3) 'We greatly doubt whether Mr. Southey's poems will be read fifty years hence; but we have no doubt whatever that they will be admired if they are read.'

In its last form the sentence is loose; in its other forms it is periodic. Notice the inversion in (1) and the two inversions in (2).

Exercise II

Synthesise the following analysed sentences:
(*Note.*—The parts of each clause are to be placed in their most effective setting, and the words in brackets to be omitted.)

1. Principal clause: Elizabeth had often told Philip
   Noun clause to pred. of prin. cl.: that she would be forced to interfere
   Adverbial clause of condition to pred. of noun cl.: unless he would take a reasonable course.

2. Principal clause: The envoy told the queen
   Noun clause to 'told': that peace was out of the question
   Adverbial clause of time to pred. of noun cl.: so long as religious liberty was made a condition.

(*Note.*—'So long' may be taken as an adverbial adjunct to the predicate of the noun clause, and the adverbial clause as one of degree. So far as composition is concerned, this is of trifling importance.)

3. Principal clause: Bengal was still governed according to the system
   Relative clause to 'system': Clive had devised which
   Adverbial clause of time to pred. of prin. cl.: when Hastings took his seat at the head of the council board.

4. Principal clause: The marquis threw the whole charge of defending it on England and Holland
   Adverbial clause of concession to pred. of prin. cl.: as the country was fertile and rich
   Relative clause to 'country': he ruled which.

5. Principal clause: He took all the liberties of an insolent servant with the government
   Relative clause to 'servant': who believes himself to be necessary
   Relative clause to 'government': he had saved which.

6. Principal clause: Thousands of busy men found every Christmas
   Noun clause to pred. of prin. cl.: that a surplus remained
   Adverbial clause of time to pred. of noun cl.: after the expenses of the year's housekeeping had been defrayed out of the year's income.

7. Principal clause: I have found an occupation in the peaceful study of birds
   Relative clause to 'occupation': which exactly falls in with the habit
   Relative clause to 'habit': I had formed (which).

8. Principal clause : A critic will undoubtedly call Temple's sentences long
   Relative clause to 'critic': who considers everything as one sentence
   Relative clause to 'everything': that lies between two full stops.

9. Principal clause : They do not express Cecil's opinions
   Adverbial clause of concession to pred. of prin. cl. : though the hand is Cecil's
   Relative clause to 'hand': these advices are written in which.

10. Principal clause : Nothing is so daintily sweet to people
    Relative clause to 'people': who are unacquainted with real calamity
    Adverbial clause of comparison to prin. cl. : as an agreeable excitement (is daintily sweet).

11. Principal clause : We saw in the last lecture
    Noun clause to pred. of prin. cl. : that the muscle changes its form
    Adverbial clause of time to pred. of noun cl. : when the nerve connected with a muscle is irritated.

12. Principal clause : The times are not always those
    Relative clause to 'times': which shine with the greatest splendour in literary history
    Relative clause to 'those': the human mind is most indebted to which.

13. Principal clause : Ben Jonson has described Bacon's eloquence in words
    Relative clause to 'words': which will bear to be quoted again
    Adverbial clause to pred. of rel. cl. : though (they have) often (been) quoted.

14. Principal clause : The council represented
    Noun clause to pred. of prin. cl. : that he would destroy her friends one by one
    Adverbial clause of condition to pred. of noun cl. : if Lennox were suffered to continue in his greatness.

15. Principal clause : Those round the queen foresaw
    Relative clause to 'those': who understood better the depth and power of religious passion
    Noun clause to pred. of prin. cl. : that the storm would sooner or later fall on England
    Adverbial clause of concession to pred. of noun cl. : however it might fare with herself.

16. Principal clause : Mr. Mill eagerly culls every expression from old despatches and minutes

Relative clause to 'expression': he can discern in which the imperfect germ of any great truth
Relative clause to 'germ' in the first rel. cl.: which has been fully developed since.

17. Principal clause: Mr. Mill never fails to bestow praise on those
Relative clause to 'those': who yet rose in a small degree above the common level of their contemporaries
Adverbial clause of concession to pred. of the rel. cl.: though (they are) far from coming up to his standard of perfection.

18. Principal clause: Every man is entitled to our gratitude and respect
Relative clause to 'man': who distinguished himself on the right side in the contest
Relative clause to 'contest' in the last clause: which divided our country in his time.

19. Principal clause: All London crowded to shout and laugh round the gibbet
Relative clause to 'gibbet': where (=on which) hung the rotting remains of a prince
Relative clause to 'prince' in the last clause: who had made England the dread of the world.

20. Principal clause: The love and awe were undiminished
Relative clause to 'love and awe': the office was regarded with which
Adverbial clause to pred. of prin. cl.: though the person of the sovereign was changed.

21. Principal clause: He at least violated it for one of the noblest ends
Relative clause to 'ends': any statesman ever had in view that
Adverbial clause of condition to pred. of prin. cl.: if James violated the constitution.

22. Principal clause: The authors of these improvements sometimes continued to recognise the principle
Adverbial clause of time to pred. of prin. cl.: while they removed a great practical evil
Relative clause to 'principle' in prin. cl.: that evil had sprung from which.

23. Principal clause: Sometimes they shrank from following it to all the conclusions
Adverbial clause of time to pred. of prin. cl.: when they had adopted a sound principle
Relative clause to 'conclusions' in prin. cl.: it would have led to which.

24. Principal clause: We do not see
   Noun clause to pred. of prin. cl.: why suppositions should be admitted into history
   Relative clause to 'suppositions' in the noun cl.: no rational man would act on which in ordinary life.

25. Principal clause: Coke was an exception to a maxim
   Relative clause to 'maxim': we believe which to be generally true
   Noun clause in apposition to 'maxim': that those are disposed to cringe to the powerful
   Relative clause to 'those' in the noun cl.: who trample on the helpless.

26. Principal clause: There is not the smallest reason to believe
   Noun clause to 'believe': that they would have prevented him from making it
   Adverbial clause of condition to pred. of noun clause to 'believe': if James and Buckingham had thought
   Noun clause to pred. of the adverbial cl.: that Bacon had a good defence.

27. Principal clause: A man must be a monster of servility and impudence
   Relative clause to 'man': who solemnly declares himself guilty of corruption to please a powerful patron
   Adverbial clause of time to pred. of rel. cl.: when he knows himself to be innocent.

28. Principal clause: It is no excuse for him
   Adverbial clause of condition to prin. cl.: if a man does that
   Relative clause to 'that' in adv. cl.: which he and all around him know to be bad
   Noun clause in apposition to 'it' in prin. cl.: that many others have done the same thing.

29. Principal clause: We firmly believe
   Noun clause to pred. of prin. cl.: that Mr. Montagu would tell us
   Adverbial clause to pred. of noun cl.: if papers were discovered
   Relative clause to 'papers' in adv. cl.: which would irresistibly prove
   Noun clause to pred. of rel. cl.: that Bacon was concerned in the poisoning of Sir Thomas Overbury
   Noun clause to 'tell' in first noun clause: that it was not thought improper in a man to put arsenic in the broth of his friend at the beginning of the seventeenth century.

30. Principal clause: We find
   Noun clause to pred. of prin. cl.: that it is also the single case
   Relative clause to 'case' in the noun cl. above: there was no gross impropriety in his receiving a present in which

Adverbial clause of time to pred. of prin. cl. : when we examine
the single case
Relative clause to 'case' in adverbial cl. : Bacon alleges in
which
Noun clause to 'alleges': that he received a present publicly.

31. Principal co-ordinate clauses A and B in copulative relation; C in adversative relation to A and B.
   - A. The dinner was pleasant
   - and
   - B. the king talked freely
   - but
   - C. he made a little speech

Adverbial clause of time to pred. of C : as it ended

Compound relative clause.
{ Relative clause to 'speech' in C: he thanked the regents in which for their devotion
Relative clause to 'speech' in C : (he) announced (in which) }

Noun clause to 'announced': that they must resign at once
Adverbial clause of cause to 'must resign': as he was now
competent to reign.

32. The Elizabethan dramatists are
{ tamper recklessly with the best feelings of human nature
and
{ not only gross in expression
but base and impure in suggestion } } too often

Relative clause to 'are gross in expression': which can be
tolerated.

33. Principal clause : The petting and the patience do little to prepare
them for the sharp discipline
Relative clause to 'discipline': which comes later
Relative clause to 'petting' : the little puppies receive which
Relative clause to 'patience': their early whims are endured with
which.

34. Principal clauses in alternative relation
{ The Duke had done something
or
he had affected something }
Relative clause to 'something': which would provide him a
resource
Adverbial clause of concession to pred. of rel. cl. : however
events might turn
Adverbial clause of condition to pred. of rel. cl. : he should be
driven to shift his colours.

35. Principal clause A: They were again in turn to exhort the laity in all the churches and cathedrals to accept the grace
Relative clause to 'grace': which was offered to them
Adverbial clause of time to pred. of prin. cl. A: when the clergy had been reconciled

and

Principal clause B in cumulative relation with A } a time was assigned
Relative clause to 'time' in B: their submissions must all be completed within which
Adverbial clause of purpose to 'was assigned' in cl. B: that they might understand
Noun clause to 'might understand': that they were not at liberty to refuse the invitation.

36. Principal clause: He sent orders
Adverbial clause of time to pred. of prin. cl.: when the poor results of the session became known to Philip
Noun clause in apposition with 'orders': that such of his Spanish suite should no longer afflict themselves with remaining in a country
Relative clause to 'country': they abhorred which
Relative clause to 'such' in the noun cl.: he had left as behind him.

37. Principal clause: The ministry seem to have felt

Noun clause to pred. of prin. clause } that it was necessary for them { to abandon and to win the confidence of the nation by some splendid and popular measure

Noun clause to 'abandon': what was supposed to be Clarendon's system
Adverbial clause of condition to 'it was necessary, etc.': if they wished to derive any advantage from Clarendon's downfall.

38. Principal clause: We infer from the great advances
Relative clause to 'advances': European society has made which in every species of knowledge, during the last four centuries

Compound noun clause to 'infer' { not that there is no more room for improvement but that immense improvements may be confidently expected in every science

Relative clause to 'science': which deserves the name.

39. Principal clause : The kindness of a venerable country gentleman was amongst the favourable influences of my early life

Compound relative clause to 'gentleman' } who had { seen a great deal of the world
and
passed many years in the practice of a laborious profession

Adverbial clause of time to pred. in compound rel. cl. : before he inherited his estates.

40. In cumulative relation. { A. Principal clause : I shared the prevailing views of the character of Henry VIII.
B. Principal clause : and it was plain.

Adverbial clause of concession to prin. cl. B : though I considered
Noun clause to 'considered' : that there might be found much to modify our censure on Cranmer's behaviour
Adverbial clause of condition to the last noun clause : if all ·the circumstances were known
Noun clause in apposition to 'it,' the subject of principal clause B : that he had gone along with the king in the most questionable actions of his reign.

THE END

BY THE SAME AUTHOR

HIGHER ARITHMETIC AND ELEMENTARY MENSURATION. Crown 8vo. 5s.

"It is an ably written treatise, eminently practical in its method and lucid in its expositions."—*Scotsman.*

"We can warmly recommend the book to our readers."—*Schoolmaster.*

"The whole is a vast storehouse of well-put matter, which should render a reader quite independent of any other text-book, and, we might say, of a teacher."—*Nature.*

". . . The examples worked out are models of clearness. Profit and loss and stocks, generally considered most difficult subjects to teach, are much simplified. There is certainly no better text-book for the arithmetic of the 'Previous' and other examinations."—*Cambridge Review.*

"In every way it comes up to our expectation of what a higher school arithmetic should be. A feature of the method is the eliciting the rule or principle from the examples given, and these examples are remarkable for their clearness and their number."—*N.Z. Schoolmaster.*

"The treatise seems to us to be most complete; the exposition lucid and thoroughly scientific, and the methods are as powerful as those of algebra up to quadratics."—*N.Z. Times.*

"We have just received the second edition, revised and enlarged, of this valuable work, and we have much pleasure in recommending it as a text-book for teachers and pupils of advanced classes.

"In the arithmetical part of the book the excellent method is adopted, not of enunciating rules, but of working out types from which the student can deduce his own rules. The work will be of great assistance to teachers of all grades in preparing either themselves or their advanced pupils for examinations. For not only, as is usual in text-books, are types of simple character solved, but also those of considerable difficulty, so that the student is well equipped for the solution of arithmetical problems.

"Where all is so good it is difficult to particularise, but the chapters on 'Ratio,' 'Proportion and Variation,' 'Surds, Approximate Calculations,' 'Progression,' and 'Scales of Notation,' deserve special mention."—*N. S. Wales Educational Gazette.*

MACMILLAN AND CO., LONDON.

KEY AND COMPANION TO "HIGHER ARITHMETIC AND ELEMENTARY MENSURATION."

Crown 8vo. 10s. net.

"This *Key and Companion* will be found of great service to teachers. We think it is a pity that the author did not call it simply a 'Companion,' for it is not a 'Key,' as that is ordinarily understood. The solution of the last example in the miscellaneous, No. 500, is very neat. This is one of the problems referring to uniformly growing grass, and Mr. Goyen solves it in a neater manner than either Hunter or Colenso."—*N. S. Wales Educational Gazette.*

"Mr. Goyen's books on arithmetic have already obtained their much-deserved celebrity in New Zealand. His methods in dealing with the various rules are concise, clear, and to the point. The *Key and Companion* should be in the hands of every teacher and of students preparing for examination. The examples in mensuration are particularly good."—*N. Z. Schoolmaster.*

"Mr. Goyen's book is a good deal more than a mere key. It not unfrequently provides alternative solutions; it supplies a sort of commentary now and then on important steps of the processes, and it occasionally diverges into corollaries and inferences of considerable use. To the ideal *selfelpista* it would, no doubt, be a Godsend."—*Saturday Review.*

"None will fail to derive advantage from a study of some of the methods used in the solutions of the problems in this key."—*Lyceum.*

"Some years ago we placed before our readers a tolerably full account of Mr. P. Goyen's *Higher Arithmetic and Elementary Mensuration*, and recommended the book to their notice as being one of unusual merit. We have now to welcome the publication of a *Key and Companion*, in which, by the omission of the easy mechanical examples of the textbook, Mr. Goyen has been able to 'set out with considerable fulness the important steps in the solutions of the problems; to give, where it seemed desirable to exemplify other aspects of the principles involved, more than one solution of a large number of problems, to emphasise important points, and to add a large amount of useful expository and other matter.' In our notice of Mr. Goyen's text-book, we expressed the opinion that he had not given sufficient prominence to the doctrine of proportion. In the *Key and Companion*, however, he has recognised that proportion is an instrument of great power; and by the use he has made of it he has shown how great is the folly of excluding it from arithmetic. Another feature of his *Key and Companion* is that in preparing it he has given great prominence to generalised equations. In the reduction of complex fractions, again, Mr. Goyen makes most effective use of the principle that the value of a fraction is not altered by multiplying its numerator and denominator by the same whole number. We may also mention the excellence of his examples in mensuration and in the handling of surd quantities. Both teachers and students working without the help of teachers will find in Mr. Goyen's *Key and Companion* a valuable and useful book."—*Australasian Schoolmaster.*

MACMILLAN AND CO., LONDON.

THE ENGLISH LANGUAGE AND LITERATURE.

HISTORICAL OUTLINES OF ENGLISH ACCIDENCE, comprising Chapters on the History and Development of the Language, and on Word-Formation. New Edition. By R. MORRIS, LL.D. Globe 8vo. 6s.

HISTORICAL LESSONS IN ENGLISH SYNTAX. By L. KELLNER, Ph.D. Companion volume to the above. Globe 8vo. 6s.

ELEMENTARY LESSONS IN HISTORICAL ENGLISH GRAMMAR, containing Accidence and Word-Formation. By R. MORRIS, LL.D. Pott 8vo. 2s. 6d.

THE OLD AND MIDDLE ENGLISH. By T. L. KINGTON OLIPHANT, M.A., Balliol College. Second Edition, Revised. Globe 8vo. Cloth. 9s.

AN OLD AND MIDDLE ENGLISH READER. On the basis of Professor JULIUS ZUPITZA'S Alt- und Mittelenglisches Uebungsbuch. With Introduction, Notes, and Glossary. By GEORGE EDWIN MACLEAN, Ph.D., Professor of the English Language and Literature in the University of Minnesota. Crown 8vo. 8s. net.

A SHAKESPEARIAN GRAMMAR. An Attempt to Illustrate some of the Differences between Elizabethan and Modern English. By the Rev. E. A. ABBOTT, D.D., formerly Headmaster of the City of London School. Extra fcap. 8vo. 6s.

SHORT STUDIES OF SHAKESPEARE'S PLOTS. By CYRIL RANSOME, Professor of Modern History and Literature, Yorkshire College, Leeds. Crown 8vo. 3s. 6d.

CHRONOLOGICAL OUTLINES OF ENGLISH LITERATURE. By F. RYLAND, M.A. Crown 8vo. 6s.

THE HISTORY OF EARLY ENGLISH LITERATURE. Being the History of English Poetry from its Beginnings to the Accession of King Ælfred. By the Rev. STOPFORD A. BROOKE, M.A. With a Map. 2 vols. 8vo. 20s. net.

A HISTORY OF ELIZABETHAN LITERATURE. 1560-1665. By GEORGE SAINTSBURY. Crown 8vo. 7s. 6d.

A HISTORY OF EIGHTEENTH CENTURY LITERATURE. 1660-1780. By EDMUND GOSSE, M.A. Crown 8vo. 7s. 6d.

MACMILLAN AND CO., LONDON.

PRIMERS

Edited by JOHN R. GREEN, M.A., LL.D. Pott 8vo. 1s. each.

ENGLISH GRAMMAR. By Rev. R. MORRIS.

ENGLISH GRAMMAR EXERCISES. By Rev. R. MORRIS and H. C. BOWEN.

EXERCISES ON MORRIS'S PRIMER OF ENGLISH GRAMMAR. By J. WETHERELL, M.A.

ENGLISH COMPOSITION. By Prof. NICHOL.

QUESTIONS AND EXERCISES IN ENGLISH COMPOSITION. By Prof. NICHOL and W. S. M'CORMICK.

PHILOLOGY. By J. PEILE, M.A.

ENGLISH LITERATURE. By Rev. STOPFORD BROOKE, M.A.

CHILDREN'S TREASURY OF LYRICAL POETRY. Selected by Prof. F. T. PALGRAVE. In two Parts. 1s. each.

A PRIMER OF CHAUCER. By ALFRED W. POLLARD.

SHAKESPEARE. By Prof. DOWDEN.

HOMER. By Right Hon. W. E. GLADSTONE.

GREEK LITERATURE. By Prof. JEBB.

ROMAN LITERATURE. By A. S. WILKINS.

MACMILLAN AND CO., LONDON.

www.ingramcontent.com/pod-product-compliance
Lightning Source LLC
Chambersburg PA
CBHW020059170426
43199CB00009B/335